# HAPPY, HAPPY, HAPPY

## My Life and Legacy as the DUCK COMMANDER

# PHIL ROBERTSON

*with* **Mark Schlabach**

HOWARD BOOKS
A DIVISION OF SIMON & SCHUSTER, INC.
New York • Nashville • London • Toronto • Sydney • New Delhi

Howard Books
A Division of Simon & Schuster, Inc.
1230 Avenue of the Americas
New York, NY 10020

First Howard Books hardcover edition May 2013

HOWARD and colophon are trademarks of Simon & Schuster, Inc.

For information about special discounts for bulk purchases,
please contact Simon & Schuster Special Sales at
1-866-506-1949 or business@simonandschuster.com.

The Simon & Schuster Speakers Bureau can bring authors to your live event.
For more information or to book an event, contact the Simon & Schuster Speakers
Bureau at 1-866-248-3049 or visit our website at www.simonspeakers.com.

Designed by Stephanie D. Walker

Manufactured in the United States of America

10  9  8  7  6  5  4  3  2  1

Library of Congress Cataloging-in-Publication Data is available.

ISBN 978-1-4767-2610-6
ISBN 978-1-4767-2611-3 (ebook)

**To my four sons: Alan, Jase, Willie, and Jep**

*"Let them revere nothing but religion, morality and liberty."*

—Excerpt from letter to Abigail Adams
from her husband John Adams regarding their two sons,
April 15, 1776

# Contents

# Contents

# HAPPY, HAPPY, HAPPY.

# HAPPY, HAPPY, HAPPY

**W**hen A&E TV approached us about doing a reality TV show based on our family, I was somewhat reluctant and wasn't quite sure if it would work.

"Let me take a guess here," I told the producers.

I told them that there was probably a boardroom meeting at the A&E headquarters in New York City, where all the suits, yuppies, and best creative minds were kicking around ideas for a new reality TV show. At some point during the meeting, someone probably spoke up and said, "Uh, Bob, I know this might sound weird, but why don't we try portraying a functional American family?"

And I'm sure the guy sitting across the table shouted, "Now, that's a novel idea!"

Everything else on TV nowadays is dysfunctional and for the most part has been that way for forty years. The last TV shows we saw that featured functional families were *The Andy Griffith Show,*

# HAPPY, HAPPY, HAPPY

*The Waltons, The Beverly Hillbillies* (don't laugh), and *Little House on the Prairie*. That was a long time ago!

I'm sure someone else in the A&E board meeting probably then asked, "Bob, where do we find a functional family in America?"

For whatever reason, they looked for one in West Monroe, Louisiana.

To be honest, our family isn't much different from other families in America. There's a mom and a dad, four grown kids, fourteen grandchildren, and a couple of great-grandkids. We started a family business, Duck Commander, which turned into a pretty lucrative enterprise with a lot of elbow grease, teamwork, and God's blessings. But as you'll find out by reading this book, we've had our share of trials and struggles, like a lot of other families. We've battled alcohol and drug abuse, sibling rivalries, and near poverty and despair at the beginning of our time together as a family. It wasn't always like what you see on TV. So except for our very manly appearances, it might not seem that we're all that different from everyone else.

But I think what separates the Robertsons from a lot of other families is our faith in God and love for each other. It's unconditional, and it has been that way for as long as I can remember. For me, the most dramatic part of every *Duck Dynasty* episode comes at the end, when our family gathers around the dinner table to

2

eat one of Miss Kay's home-cooked meals. You don't see families gathering up like that anymore. Everybody in America is so busy, busy, busy. Americans are too preoccupied with their cell phones and computers, so they don't take the time to sit down with their spouses, children, grandchildren, aunts and uncles, and grandparents to eat a meal together. The family structure is slipping away from America, but not in our house.

Thomas Jefferson, the third president of the United States, probably said it best. Shortly after our founding fathers left the large cities of Europe for the wide-open spaces of America, Jefferson said of the American people, "When they get piled upon one another in large cities, as in Europe, they will become corrupt as in Europe." You'll never find me living in a city, folks. Where I live, I am 911. Like I say, if you spend too much time in the subdivision, you go a-runnin' when the snakes fall out of trees!

> What separates the Robertsons from a lot of other families is our faith in God and love for each other.

The other problem in America today is that the young girls don't know how to cook. Their grandmothers and mamas cooked for them, but they never took the time to learn how to cook. They were more interested in other things. If you go out into the subdivisions and suburbs of America, where all of the yuppies live, you'll see the restaurants are packed with people.

They don't want to eat slop and they're looking for good food, but they don't want to take the time to make it. Dad is working, Mom is working, and so no one has the time or energy to cook a good meal anymore. So our families end up eating in restaurants, where they're surrounded by noise and clutter, instead of sharing quality time in a family setting.

When I reluctantly agreed to be a part of *Duck Dynasty,* the producers told me they were going to make a reality show without duck hunting. I asked them if they understood that I spend most of my waking hours in a duck blind or in the woods. There isn't much else I do! I asked the producers, "You know, you're dealing with a bunch of rednecks who duck-hunt. For the life of me, do you really think this is going to work?"

"Ozzy Osbourne made it," they told me.

Ozzy was able to pull it off on reality TV, so he's given hope to all of us. I'd never really watched many reality TV shows and knew nothing about them, but I was 100 percent convinced *Duck Dynasty* would never work. It just goes to show how little I know about today's world, because I was dead wrong. For the life of me, I can't figure out why people are so attracted to our family. Maybe it's because we live our lives like people really want to live, how we all used to live before everything got so busy, busy, busy.

*Duck Dynasty* has made us a little bit more famous, but it hasn't changed much of anything about us. Miss Kay and I still live in the same house on the Ouachita River outside of West Monroe, and I'm still driving the same truck and hunting with the same guns and dogs. Of course, we still go to church every Sunday morning and I'm still reading my Bible. If anything has changed, it's that it's a little more difficult to go places, like driving down an interstate or walking through an airport. If I'm driving somewhere, someone might drive by and recognize me (undoubtedly because of my beard). They'll get on a cell phone and call their friends, and then when I stop to take a leak, I'll have to sign autographs and pose for pictures for about thirty minutes.

When we went duck-hunting in Arkansas recently, we stopped at a Walmart to buy our out-of-state hunting licenses. We were in the sporting goods section of the store when some people recognized us, so we started posing for pictures and signing T-shirts. When it was finally time for us to leave, three African-American girls approached us.

"Well, girls, I didn't know you soul sisters were duck hunters," I told them.

"We don't care about no ducks," one of them said. "You're ZZ Top, ain't you?"

I guess not everyone in America watches *Duck Dynasty*.

Miss Kay and I haven't done too badly, and the good Lord has really blessed us. We've been married nearly fifty years and our boys have grown up to become loving husbands and fathers, the kind of men I wanted them to be. Our business is in good shape, even after I had my doubts about where it was going. But when the boys took over, they breathed new life into it, and it's still growing. Not many are as fortunate as we are, with all the trouble in the world.

Since I turned over the reins of my company to my sons, I keep busy with hunting and fishing and speaking engagements. God provided those. The appearances give me an opportunity to preach the gospel, which I feel compelled to do. I've also had a chance to learn from all the people I've met—and the chance to travel all over the country. I hope I've helped those who have heard the gospel.

Where do I go from here? The time is near when the dust will return to the earth and the spirit to God who gave it. I'm ready for that, but not quite yet. I have a lot of speeches to give, a lot of blinds to build, a lot of *Duck Dynasty* episodes to make, and who knows how many more duck seasons to hunt.

Maybe the greatest thing is that I've been able to live life the way I wanted. Following Jesus has been a blast. The Lord has blessed me mightily.

It is what makes me happy, happy, happy.

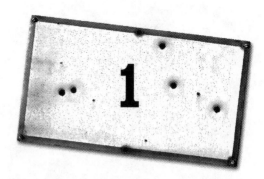

# LOW-TECH MAN

*Rule No. 1 for Living Happy, Happy, Happy*
Simplify Your Life
(Throw Away Your Cell Phones and Computers, Yuppies)

**W**hat ever happened to the on-and-off switch? I don't ask for much, but my hope is that someday soon we'll get back to where we have a switch that says on and off. Nowadays, everything has a pass code, sequence, or secret decoder. I think maybe the yuppies overdid it with these computers. The very thing they touted as the greatest time-saving device in history—a computer—now occupies the lion's share of everybody's life.

Here's a perfect example: I owned a Toyota Tundra truck for a while, and I got tired of driving around with my headlights on all the time. If I'm driving around in the woods and it's late in the evening, I don't want my headlights on. I tried to turn the lights off and couldn't do it. I spent an hour inside the truck with a friend of mine trying to turn off the lights, but we never figured it out. So I called the car dealer, and he told me to look in the owner's manual. Well, it wasn't in the book, which is about as thick as a Bible. Finally, about ten days later, after my buddy spent some time with a bunch of young bucks in town driving Toyota trucks, he told me he had the code for turning off my lights.

Now, get this: First, you have to shut off the truck's engine. Then you have to step on the emergency brake with your left foot until you hear one click. Not two clicks—only one. If you hear two clicks, you have to bring the brake back up and start all over. After you hear one click, you crank the engine back up. I sat there thinking, *Why would you possibly need a code for turning off head-lights?* What kind of mad scientist came up with that sequence? Seriously, what kind of mind designs something like that? To me, it's not logical. I just don't get it, but that's where we are in today's world.

I miss the times when life was simple. I came from humble, humble beginnings. When I was a young boy growing up in the far northwest corner of Louisiana, only about six miles from Texas and ten miles from Arkansas, we didn't have very much in terms of personal possessions. But even when times were the hardest, I never once heard my parents, brothers, or sisters utter the words "Boy, we're dirt-poor."

We never had new cars, nice clothes, or much money, and we

certainly never lived in an extravagant home, but we were always happy, happy, happy, no matter the circumstances. My daddy, James Robertson, was that kind of a guy. He didn't care about all the frills in life; he was perfectly content with what we had and so were we. We were a self-contained family, eating the fruits and vegetables that grew in our garden or what the Almighty provided us in other ways. And, of course, when we were really lucky, we had meat from the deer, squirrels, fish, and other game my brothers and I hunted and fished in the areas around our home, along with the pigs, chickens, and cattle we raised on our farm.

It was the 1950s when I was a young boy, but we lived about like it was the 1850s. My daddy always reminded us that when he was a boy, his family would go to town and load the wagon down and return home with a month's worth of necessities. For only five dollars, they could buy enough flour, salt, pepper, sugar, and other essentials to survive for weeks. We rarely went to town for groceries, probably because we seldom had five dollars to spend, let alone enough gas to get there!

> We rarely went to town for groceries, probably because we seldom had five dollars to spend, let alone enough gas to get there!

I grew up in a little log cabin in the woods, and it was located far from Yuppieville. The cabin was built near the turn of the twentieth century and was originally a three-room shotgun house. At some point, someone added a small, protruding shed room off the southwest corner of the house. The room had a door connecting to the main room, which is where the fireplace was located. I guess whoever added the room thought it would be warmest near the fireplace, which was the only source of heat in our house. In hindsight, it really didn't make a difference where you put the room if you didn't insulate or finish the interior walls. It was going to be cold in there no matter what.

I slept in the shed with my three older brothers—Jimmy Frank, the oldest, who was ten years older than me; Harold, who was six years older than me; and Tommy, who was two years older than me. I never thought twice about sleeping with my three brothers in a bed; I thought that's what everybody did. My younger brother, Silas, slept in the main room on the west end of the house because he had a tendency to wet the bed. My older sister, Judy, also slept in that room.

I can still remember trying to sleep in that room during the winter—there were a lot of sleepless nights. The overlapping boards on the exterior walls of the house were barely strong enough to block the wind, and they sure didn't stand a chance against freezing temperatures. The shed room was about ten square feet, and its only furnishings were a standard bed and battered chest of drawers. My brothers and I kept a few pictures, keepsakes, and whatnots on the two-by-four crosspieces on the framing of the interior walls. Every night before bed, we unloaded whatever was in our pockets, usually a fistful of marbles and whatever else we'd found that day, on the crosspieces and then reloaded our pockets again the next morning.

To help battle the cold, my brothers and I layered each other in heavy homemade quilts on the bed. Jimmy Frank and Harold were the biggest, so they slept on opposite sides of the bed, with Tommy and me sleeping in between them. My daddy and my mother, Merritt Robertson (we started calling them Granny and Pa when our children were born), slept in a small middle room in the house. My youngest sister, Jan, was the baby of the family and slept in a crib next to my parents' bed until she was old enough to sleep with Judy.

The fireplace in the west room was the only place to get warm. It was made of the natural red stone of the area and was rather large. One of my brothers once joked that it was big enough to "burn up a wet mule." Because the fireplace was the only source of heat in the home, it was my family's gathering spot. Every morning in the winter, the first person out of bed—it always seemed to be Harold—was responsible for starting a fire. It would usually reignite with pine fatwood kindling, but sometimes you had to blow the coals to stoke the flames. Some of my favorite memories as a child were when we baked potatoes and roasted hickory nuts on the fireplace coals for snacks. We usually ate them with some of my mother's homemade dill pickles. There was never any candy or junk food in our house.

The only other room in the cabin was a combination kitchen and dining area. The cookstove was fueled by natural gas from a well that was located down the hill and across the creek. The pressure from the well was so low that it barely produced enough gas to cook. Pa always said we were lucky to have the luxury of running water in the house, even if it was only cold water coming through a one-inch pipe from a hand-dug well to the kitchen sink. We didn't even have a bathtub or commode in the house! The water pipeline habitually froze during the winter, and my brothers and I spent many mornings unfreezing the pipe with hot coals from the fire. When the pipe was frozen, we'd grab a shovelful of coals and place them on the ground under the pipe. When we finally heard gurgling and then water spitting out of the kitchen sink, we knew we could return to the fire to get warm again.

Breakfast began when Granny put a big pot of water on the stove to heat. We didn't have a hot-water heater, so we bathed in cold water when I was young. Granny used the hot water for cooking and cleaning the dishes. Breakfast usually consisted of hot buttermilk biscuits, blindfolded fried eggs, butter, and fresh "sweet milk": every morning, one of my brothers or I would take a pail of hot water to the barn to clean the cows' udders after we milked them. There were always several jars of jams and jellies on our table. Pa and Granny canned them from wild fruits that grew in abundance in the Arklatex area. Pa liked to scold us for having too many jars open at once; he said we opened them just to hear the Ball jar lids pop. He may have been right.

Nearly everything we ate came from our land. The eggs came from our chickens, the milk and butter from our cows. Bacon and sausage came from the hogs we raised and butchered. We canned vegetables from our large garden, which spread over about eight acres in three different patches. Cucumbers were turned into jars and jars of sweet, sour, bread-and-butter, and dill pickles. Our pantry shelves were lined with canned tomatoes, peppers, beets, and just about anything else my family grew, including pears, peaches, plums, and grapes, as well as the abundant dewberries and blackberries of the area. Cut-up cabbage, green tomatoes, onions, and peppers were mixed together and canned to make what we called chow-chow, a relish that was a delicious accompaniment to just about anything—especially fish.

In addition to our garden, where we also grew such things as English peas, butter and pole beans, lettuce, turnips, mustard greens, onions, radishes, carrots, Irish and sweet potatoes, cantaloupes, and watermelons, my family grew several fields of peas, peanuts, and corn. We started many of the vegetables from seeds that were planted in a hotbed (called a cold frame by some) in early February. My brothers and I gathered cow and horse manure, which, as it decomposed, kept the bed warm and enriched the soil. After the plants sprouted and grew big enough, we transferred them to the garden.

One year Pa, figuring he would get a jump on the market for the early watermelons that brought the highest prices, had my brothers and I collect manure from the cow pens to put into two hundred holes. He directed us to dig the holes two feet square and two feet deep. In early February, Jimmy Frank and Harold laboriously filled washtub after washtub with manure and then transported them on a slide pulled by an old mule to the holes that were dug. After depositing the manure into the holes, we mixed the top of it with soil and planted the watermelon seeds.

To be perfectly honest, Tommy and I didn't become too interested in the project until Jimmy Frank and Harold told us we should plant marbles—along with the watermelon seeds—in the holes. They promised us we would grow a big crop of marbles. Of course, we were young enough—and thus gullible enough—to believe them. We already had marbles running out our ears from ill-gotten gains at the schoolyard, where we played bull's-eye, cat's-eye, and hotbox for "keeps" (whoever shot best and won the others' marbles got to keep them). We won regularly and often came home with pockets bulging with marbles, which we deposited in a five-gallon bucket just inside the back door. Tommy and I grabbed our bucket and, with high hopes, planted them in the manure just like our older brothers told us to do.

It didn't take Tommy or me too long to realize we had been duped. We ended up sacrificing ammunition for our slingshots for a bumper crop that never came. There were always two things in my pocket when I was young—marbles and a slingshot. We made our slingshots from forked tree limbs and red real-rubber bands we cut from old inner tubes (the black synthetic inner tubes didn't have the necessary snap to propel a marble or small rock). We used the slingshots to bring down small birds, but Granny and my grandmothers always admonished us not to shoot the mockingbirds or "redbirds," as they called cardinals.

Our watermelons came up beautifully that year. The decaying manure heated the beds enough to sprout the seeds early, and the soil's added richness gave the young watermelon plants a tremendous growth spurt that turned the hillside where they were growing into a couple of acres of lush, verdant green vines. Pa never followed up on selling them, so we wound up giving away what we didn't eat to kinfolk and friends.

My entire family took part in harvesting fruits and vegetables. If we hadn't, we wouldn't have had enough to eat. From the beginning of May, when the mayhaws and dewberries ripened, until the end of fall, with the gathering of muscadines and pears, my family and I could regularly be found in the area's swamps, fields, forests, and abandoned home sites. With our buckets and tubs, from the youngest to the oldest, we would be stooped over or stretched upward gathering whatever fruit was in season.

Pa, who worked on drilling rigs usually located in the wilds, often discovered fruit trees and berry and grape vines as he moved about with the rigs. He also knew the locations of many old home sites with abandoned peach orchards, grapevines, and plum and pear trees. There was no shortage of places to harvest. The trick was to get there when the fruit was ripe—and before another family beat you to it!

> The trick was to get there when the fruit was ripe—and before another family beat you to it!

I remember one particularly cold, wet spring when my family was wading ankle-deep (in our everyday shoes because we didn't have rubber boots) to gather mayhaws in cottonmouth-infested waters near Myrtis, Louisiana, in a swampy area off Black Bayou. Clouds of mosquitoes covered our backs, biting through our thin shirts while we stooped to gather the floating fruit we shook from thickly clustered trees. Mayhaw jelly is still my favorite, and even today my wife, Kay, and I gather the bright reddish-orange berries from the swamps around our home each spring. We make plenty of the tart jelly for our needs, usually with enough left over for our children and other family members and friends. Mayhaw jelly has a unique, delicious flavor.

One year when I was young, the wild grapes were so abundant in the old Ruby Florence field that they filled all of our tubs and buckets with rich, purple-red fruit. We could barely fit our harvest into the car, which was already crowded with adults and children. In fact, the trunk was so crammed full of tubs and buckets of fruit piled on top of each other that the lid wouldn't shut. Several large buckets and pans of grapes were jammed inside the car, on the floorboards, between our legs, and on our laps. The harvest was so great that Granny lit all four burners on the stove and had Pa and Jimmy Frank set an entire number three washtub full of grapes on top of them to render the juice.

As our luck would have it, this was also one of the years when the price of sugar was sky-high (always a consideration in canning as to whether it was worth the cost). After making a smaller amount of jelly than usual, my family simply sealed a number of gallons of surplus grape juice in quart jars without sugar and stored them in the cabinets alongside and beneath the sink—thinking we might make jelly later, after the price of sugar went down. But we eventually found that the stored juice was delicious, so my brothers and I drank a quart or more daily for breakfast and snacks. Before too long, the juice began to ferment. In only a short time, it turned into a very good wine. My parents and older relatives began to drink this, too, but couldn't finish it before it turned into vinegar. Granny used the vinegar in her canning throughout the rest of the year.

Of course, man can't survive on fruits and vegetables alone (at least not a *real* man), so we also raised and butchered our own beef, usually killing two steer calves annually that weighed about four hundred pounds each. The calves were the offspring of our milk cows, which were bred to my aunt Myrtle's beef-type bull—a runty, mostly Black Angus mix, which still sired nice calves. Pa and my older brothers would kill the calf, gut and skin it, and wrap it in an old bedsheet, which they then put into the trunk of our car. We didn't have a deep-freezer, so the meat was taken to Vivian, Louisiana, about two miles away, where it was hung to cool and age in a local icehouse. After about fourteen days, Pa brought the sides of beef home and cut them up on the dining table. Then Granny and Pa wrapped the meat in freezer paper and took it to a rental storage locker in town, where it was frozen. Granny periodically retrieved packages of beef when she was in town and transferred them to the small freezing compartment in the refrigerator at home.

Homegrown chickens were another staple at my house when I was a boy. Pa bought two hundred baby chicks by mail order each year at a cost of about five dollars per hundred—one hundred early and another hundred later, so we always had young fryers running around the yard. It was a big day when the baby chicks were brought home from the post office in a ventilated cardboard box. They were immediately moved into a brooder Jimmy Frank built with four-by-eight-foot sheets of tin. The brooder was heated by using an old washtub—with vents on the sides—and a small burner that was fueled by the natural gas well that also heated the stove.

We didn't wait too long to start eating the chickens—even if it took eight of them to make a meal! We usually kept twenty or so hens every year to lay eggs, and we dined on the older ones from previous years during the winter. Of course we cooked and prepared them the old-fashioned way: wringing their necks, plucking the feathers, and singeing them over a stove burner. Our Sunday meals in the spring and summer typically consisted of fried chicken and homemade ice cream, which was made with the rich cream of our Jersey cows. On the way home from church, we'd pick up a twenty-five-pound block of ice, and my brothers and I would make the ice cream outside. Jimmy Frank or Harold cranked the freezer, while Tommy or I sat on it to keep it steady.

The story of the Robertson family is a pretty good picture of an early American family. We didn't have much, but we loved each other and found ways to keep each other entertained. We didn't have cell phones or computers, but somehow we managed to survive. As far as I know, none of my brothers or sisters has ever owned a cell phone, and Jimmy Frank is the only one who owns a computer, because he's a newspaperman and needs one to write his stories. I've never owned a cell phone and don't plan on ever having one. I've never owned a computer, and I'm still trying to figure out what the fuss over social media is all about. I can promise you one thing: you'll never find me on Twitter or Skype. If anyone needs to talk to me, they know where I live.

# GREAT OUTDOORS

*Rule No. 2 for Living Happy, Happy, Happy*
Don't Let Your Grandkids Grow Up to Be Nerds

**T**he Boy Scouts might have the motto "Be Prepared," but where I grew up, you practically went straight from diapers to manhood. You had to be prepared for anything. I learned to hunt and fish shortly after I learned to walk. If you couldn't shoot and kill something, chances were you weren't going to eat. If a hurricane had hit my boyhood home and wiped out everything, I would have found a way to survive—even when I was only five years old! I'm trying to teach those same lessons of survival to my grandchildren, because the last thing I want is for them to grow up to be nerds.

Let me tell you one thing: I don't see the inherent value in the video games that kids are playing today. But that's all these kids seem to want to do. Kids in America today are overweight and lazy, and it's their parents' fault for letting it happen. Kids sit around playing video games and eating junk food all day, and when they're not doing that, they're texting on their cell phones. It's only their fingers that are moving; they're not getting out and about. Have you ever seen a macho man walking around with a cell phone, mashing it with his fingers and yakking on it all day? That's too much talking. By the time these kids are young adults, they're going to have to go to Walmart to buy a personality. Kids need to be out with nature, learning what it takes to survive in this world.

> By the time these kids are young adults, they're going to have to go to Walmart to buy a personality.

When I was a very young boy, much of our food and sustenance came from the land around us. While living in Vivian, Louisiana, immediately following World War II and before we moved into the log cabin where I spent my formative years, Granny often told us, "If we have another depression, we could live off this acre." The Great Depression was never far from my parents' thoughts; they suffered through the worst economic depression to ever hit the United States when they were younger.

In those days, living off the land surrounding our house sounded feasible. Even on our limited acreage, we had a milk cow that was pastured on half the land and staked out alongside the road when grass was scarce. We had several fruit trees, which we'd planted, along with a large truck garden (it was called a "truck garden" because the overflow of what we raised in it was put on a truck and taken to town to sell), that provided abundantly from spring to fall. The garden yielded such food as turnips and greens far into the mild Louisiana winters. My great-aunt Willie Mae Irvins, who lived next door to us, kept a flock of chickens, and we purchased eggs and occasional young fryers and roasting hens from her.

As a boy, living off the land influenced my outlook on life probably more than anything else, especially after I discovered an abundance of wild game and fish that was there for the taking in the area where we lived. I always had a conviction that I could survive off the land without being tied to a regular job. As I grew older, that belief influenced many of my decisions.

> I always had a conviction that I could survive off the land without being tied to a regular job.

I killed my first duck—actually, two of them—when I was eleven years old. I was hunting on the bank of a small slough when three teal and a pintail flew close enough for me to shoot. I fired three times, bringing down the pintail and one teal. To this day, I can show you the exact spot where I shot those ducks. Remember what I said about being prepared? If I ever go back there, I'll be sure to take my dog or a boat, or at least some good waders. My first kill taught me a valuable lesson—sometimes shooting the ducks isn't nearly as hard as retrieving them!

With no retriever and no boat, the only way I could recover the birds was to take off my blue jeans and tattered shirt and wade into the icy water. I returned home with them and proudly announced to my father, "I have struck!" (As you might have noticed, I sometimes speak in dramatic terms if the occasion warrants it.) It turned out the event was momentous: it shaped the rest of my life and absolutely convinced me I could live off the land.

My father always lived by that philosophy and passed it on to my brothers and me. The son of Judge Euan Robertson, longtime Vivian justice of the peace, Pa grew up a farm boy outside of town, with two brothers and four sisters. He gravitated early to a career in the oil industry, which was booming with the fabulous East Texas and Pine Island discoveries, both classified as giant oil fields, practically at his doorstep.

Pa served in the U.S. Navy at San Diego during World War II, achieving the rank of fireman first class. His familiarity with heavy pumps, which he gained in the oil fields, pointed him toward the repair base, where he fixed even bigger pumps used in warships. After returning home from the war, Pa bought a house on an acre of land just outside of Vivian with a federal homeowner's loan. It was a small A-frame house, with two bedrooms, located close to town and Highway 2. I was born at a clinic in Vivian on April 24, 1946. I was named after Granny's first cousin Phil Shores, who was killed in World War II, and my great-grandfather Lemuel Alexander Shores (my middle name is Alexander).

I think much of my independent attitude was fostered by the fine example of Aunt Willie Mae next door. She was part of the original Robertson clan that moved to northwest Louisiana from Tennessee in a covered wagon in the late 1800s. (In fact, there's a street in Nashville—James Robertson Parkway—that is named after one of my early ancestors. He was an explorer and companion of Daniel Boone and cofounded the city of Nashville.) Willie Mae was eleven years old at the time and lived long enough to tell her grandchildren and numerous great-nieces and -nephews about making the trip.

Willie Mae's husband had been dead for many years before we moved next to her, but he left her with a few acres of land and a little money, which she used to build cabins she then rented out. With that income and more from boarders in two of the rooms in her home, and with a garden, chickens, and a milk cow, she made out pretty well. She often hired my siblings and me to weed her garden, mow her yard, and complete any other chores she could think up. We were paid with a shiny dime (she saved every one she acquired and had a considerable hoard), which just so happened to be the price of admission to the picture show.

Saturday afternoon trips to the double features at the local movie theater were about our only form of entertainment. We didn't have a TV, so we crowded around a radio near the fireplace to listen to Roy Rogers and Gene Autry. I'll never forget the opening monologue of *Gunsmoke,* when the announcer would introduce "the story of the violence that moved west with young America, and the story of a man who moved with it." Then Marshal Matt Dillon, with his deep, resonant voice, would proclaim, "I'm that man, Matt Dillon, United States marshal, the first man they look for and the last they want to meet." I used to love hearing those words.

> We were paid with a shiny dime, which just so happened to be the price of admission to the picture show.

After a few years of living next door to Aunt Willie Mae, my mother began urging my father to move to a larger place outside of town. Granny grew up in the country and thought it would be easier to raise her family there. There were six kids in our family after my youngest brother, Si, was born, so we needed more space in the house, too. Her biggest concern was there was a busy paved highway that ran in front of our house, and my mama always worried one of her children would wander into traffic, with the dangerous speed limit of twenty-five miles per hour. After one of my brothers was nearly hit by a speeding car, she ordered Pa to find us another place to live.

Granny wanted to buy the old Douglas Waters place, a log home that sat on about twenty acres between Vivian and Hosston, Louisiana. It was on the same road that ran in front of our old house, but the Waters home sat several hundred yards back, making it much safer for my siblings and me. But Pa wasn't interested in buying it, so we instead moved into a rental home in the middle of the Pine Island oil field. It was located ten miles south of Vivian, and we had an oil well right in the middle of our front yard. The oil field ruined our water, which stained our commodes and sinks. The water smelled and tasted bad. Our drinking water came from a cistern made from an old oil field tank that collected water off the roof. It didn't take Granny and Pa long to realize we had to find somewhere else to live.

About a year later, we ended up moving into a log home that used to be owned by the Waters family—the log home Granny had wanted to purchase all along, which was where I would spend my formative years and was the house I told you about earlier. My great-aunt Myrtle Gauss bought the house because the place adjoined her four hundred acres of land. We rented the house from her, and she put us in charge of tending to her seven cows and bull, an old mule named Jake, and an equally old (and stubborn) horse named Dolly. She rented us the house and her four hundred acres of land for the kinfolk price of twenty dollars a month.

Moving to that log home enabled my father to recapture his youth, which in turn shaped the lives of my brothers and me. The old Waters place had about twenty acres of land, only ten of which, around the house, was cleared and tillable land. A creek that flowed year-round traversed the rest of the land, meandering across Aunt Myrtle's four hundred acres and providing ample water for our stock. Our land, which included a mature growth of oak, hickory, pine, sweet gum, and a variety of other trees, adjoined Aunt Myrtle's property. On her land were two cleared, cultivatable fields of about thirty acres each. Mature woods covered the rest of the property. A wide pipeline right-of-way cut across all the land, which, because of its maintenance and mowing, grew a lot of grass that provided pasturage for the animals. The right-of-way also accommodated electric and telephone lines. A barbed-wire fence enclosed the entire four hundred and twenty acres and was a constant chore for us to repair and maintain.

Doing things the way they were done while he was growing up enabled Pa to make our farm self-sufficient in many ways—we were still living as people did in the 1800s, although it was a hundred years later. About forty acres of the land were worked with the old mule (and later a gift horse named Dan) and hand plows to produce a great deal of our food, plus grain and fodder for the horses, cows, hogs, and chickens. The fields and wooded parts of the farm yielded squirrels, quail, and doves; ducks and fish were easily obtainable from Black Bayou, only a couple of miles away. An occasional trip to Caddo Lake produced catches of white perch and bream. Our out-of-pocket expenses were minimal.

Some lagniappe came from a boom in fur pelts. My brothers and I were able to get a couple of steel traps and set them out on the creeks running throughout our land. "There's a mink walking every creek in Louisiana" was a popular saying at the time, and an extra-large prime pelt would bring thirty-five dollars—a big sum for a youth, just for the fun of trapping. We never made much money with our too-few traps, but we learned a lot about wildlife in our pursuit of mink, raccoon, and opossum pelts.

My developmental years also coincided with Pa's advancement in the oil fields as he progressed from roughneck, driller, and tool pusher to drilling superintendent for a series of small companies. He was a good hand and in his prime. His skills were in enough demand to allow him to shift from job to job easily. When a company for which he was working idled its rigs, he would go to work for another that hadn't. But he still suffered occasional layoffs—which were sometimes prolonged enough to cause hardship. Granny complained that he always seemed to get laid off during duck season, enabling him to hunt more. He took it all in stride. His attitude could be summed up in a phrase he often used: "I was looking for a job when I got this one."

There were lots of chores on the farm, with my older brothers doing the plowing and tending of the larger animals. Jimmy Frank did the milking, and Harold fed the hogs. The younger children fed the chickens and did the lighter work. Judy did most of her work inside, and the cooking experience she gained would be enhanced later with dishes such as jambalaya and white beans that she learned how to cook while living in south Louisiana.

Granny complained that he always seemed to get laid off during duck season, enabling him to hunt more.

Growing up on the farm wasn't all work—we learned to have a lot of fun, too, and transformed our land into our own massive playground. In the front yard we regularly spent hours playing a game we devised using a broomstick or a broken hoe handle for a bat and several discarded socks stuffed tightly into one another for a ball. The game was a combination of baseball and dodgeball. Once you hit the sock ball into play, it could be picked up and thrown at you. If you hadn't reached base or strayed too far from it and were hit with the sock ball, you were out. The rest of the rules were those of conventional baseball.

Jimmy Frank, by virtue of being the eldest brother by four years, was umpire, coach, and general arbiter of play—not without some objections and arguments from his brothers and cousins. It was he who decided to let me bat left-handed, although I threw right-handed. He made all of my other brothers put the broomstick on their right shoulder.

Granny's once-attractive front yard, which was surrounded by several mature oak trees with rock-walled flower beds around them, was turned into a beaten-down ball field with fairly large holes in the sandy soil around the bases—the result of years of my brothers and me and our friends and relatives sliding into them. Although my four brothers and I were usually enough for a pretty good game, frequently our friends, such as Mac, John Paul, Marv Hobbs, Frankie Hale, or Kenny Tidwell, joined us. Even Pa, Judy, and Jan were occasional participants.

Our backyard served as a football field—complete with a goalpost at one end, which Jimmy Frank and Harold made from a couple of oak-tree uprights and a sweet-gum crossbar. Remarkably, that football field ended up becoming the proving ground for several North Caddo High School Rebels and later Louisiana Tech University Bulldogs players.

Our football field was bounded by a couple of big oak trees on the east, the log house on the north, the smokehouse and outhouse on the south, and a vegetable garden on the west. It was about thirty yards long and half as wide. We played two-hands-below-the-waist touch football year-round. Jimmy Frank, who played for the Vivian High School Warriors until it was consolidated into the North Caddo High School, always had a plentiful supply of footballs—old worn ones from his high school team.

Jimmy Frank played center his freshman year, making first string when a player ahead of him quit school to join the navy during the Korean conflict. Jimmy Frank was later moved to guard, then tackle (all 147 pounds of him) during his senior year, where he made second-team all-district. Jimmy Frank played linebacker all four years—players still played both offense and defense during those days—but he really wanted to be a quarterback. Since Jimmy Frank couldn't do it, he was going to make sure one of us would play in the backfield.

Since we played on a short field in our backyard, each team had only four downs to score, or the ball went over. I remember Jimmy Frank slapping our hands when we missed a pass, and then smacking the ball into our belly and saying, "Catch it." Everyone learned to throw. I started passing when my hands were so small that I was unable to grip the ball fully and had to balance it on my palm.

My brothers and our friends had varying abilities when it came to football. Tommy was the first to make quarterback, later converting to halfback to make room for me when I began playing for North Caddo High. Passing seemed to come naturally for me. Harold, who had a milk allergy and underwent two major operations while a child, suffered a broken elbow while playing freshman football and never played in high school. Silas was a hard-hitting defensive back for the Rebels. Tommy and I earned first-team all-district football honors. As a senior, I was named first-team all-state quarterback and first-team all-district outfield in baseball.

When I graduated from high school, I followed Tommy to Louisiana Tech in Ruston, Louisiana, on a full football scholarship. Tommy started as a wide receiver for Louisiana Tech but was converted to cornerback his junior year. I sat on the sidelines my first year, then earned the starting quarterback job as a redshirt freshman the next year.

Playing college football wouldn't have been nearly the same without having one of my brothers there with me. We were all intensely competitive, and this trait extended to all our activities, not just

> My brothers and I were intensely competitive, and this trait extended to all our activities, not just sports.

sports. We played for blood, whether it was Monopoly, dominoes, or card games. We showed no mercy, and tenderhearted Jan, who often cried in frustration, was not consoled but ridiculed. In fact, we went out of our way to tease her and make her cry.

Our competitiveness may have reached its peak in the waging of our "Corncob Wars." One side took up a position inside the barn, while the other attacked from outside. We used corncobs, of which there were plenty in the barn; feed troughs; and the barnyard during the winter months. A hit from a corncob below the waist rendered a player "dead," and he had to withdraw from the game. When everyone on one side had been "killed," the remaining players on the other side had won.

Some little quirks in the game made it noteworthy. Although you could keep playing if a corncob hit you above the waist, you had better not stick your head out from behind cover or you risked a knot on your noggin. You were fair game for a well-aimed cob, whether or not it "killed" you.

Necessity also added another messy detail. In the late spring and summer, corncobs became scarce around the barn, but there were always plenty of dried cow chips. These became legal missiles, too. If you found one that was crusted over enough to pick up but still soft on the inside, you were a force to be feared. We still laugh about a wet patty that got Jimmy Frank full in the face. Luckily, he was wearing his glasses.

We also played a game in which we would wrench old, dried cornstalks from the ground and square off like sword fighters in a duel. One would hold his stalk out, and the other would strike and try to break it. If he failed, the other was required to hold his stalk out and let it be smashed. Whoever survived with an intact cornstalk, usually after repeated smashes, was the winner.

I guess now I know why my sons are so darned competitive—they learned it from their father. My brothers and I spent our youth competing with each other outdoors; there weren't any Xbox 360 or Nintendo games to keep us occupied inside. I spent my youth exploring the fields, woods, and swamps that surrounded our home. My time out in nature shaped the rest of my life, and it's something I wanted to make sure my sons learned to enjoy. Whether it was hunting, fishing, or playing sports, my children were going to grow up outside. They weren't going to be sitting on the couch inside.

At least they didn't grow up to be nerds.

# RISE, KILL, AND EAT

*Rule No. 3 for Living Happy, Happy, Happy*
Learn to Cook (It's Better than Eating Slop)

**H**ere's a fact: every human being on Earth has to eat or they will die. It's called starvation. You have to eat if you're a human being, whether you live in Monroe, Louisiana, or in some foreign land, like Los Angeles or New York. There has to be a food supply, and you have to consume food or you're dead. It's an undeniable fact—look it up.

Not everyone likes to eat. These little chicks today are starving themselves to death, which is kind of ironic, but it's their choice. Since you have to eat to live, you're left with a dilemma. You can choose not to learn how to cook and just eat slop, and you'll stay alive. You can live off terrible cooking, which doesn't taste very good, but you'll somehow manage to survive. But my contention is that if you have to eat anyway, it just seems to me that you're shortchanging yourself if you don't learn how to cook. If you have to eat, why not learn how to eat well?

Of course, the downside to eating well is that if you eat too much, you can't get through the door. Well, if that happens, you might ought to cut back some. You can overdo anything, and when you can't get through the door because you're too rotund, you might ought to say, "I think I need to start eating a few salads." I'm not saying you should just shovel it in. I'm just saying if you learn how to cook, your stay on Earth might be more enjoyable.

I learned to cook when I was young, and most of my meals started with something I killed. I have a God-given right to pursue happiness, and happiness to me is killing things, skinning them, plucking them, and then having a good meal. What makes me happy is going out and blowing a duck's head off. As it says in Acts 10:13 (KJV), "And there came a voice to him, Rise, Peter; kill, and eat."

> What makes me happy is going out and blowing a duck's head off.

Rise, kill, and eat—that's my modus operandi.

When I was young, heaven to me was hunting in the woods around our house or fishing on the nearby lakes and rivers. We hunted and threw lines into the Red River for catfish and white perch nearly every day. We didn't have much of a choice; it's where we got our next meal.

## Rise, Kill, and Eat

But when I was in high school, we were forced to move out of the log cabin where I grew up. My aunt Myrtle sold the farm, so we moved to the nearby town of Dixie, Louisiana. The town was a nice enough place; we lived on Main Street, just a stone's throw from Stroud's General Store, which was adjoined by a one-room post office. The general store and a cotton gin were the only businesses in town.

My father hoped the change of environment would help my mother, who had suffered a nervous breakdown and needed numerous trips to Schumpert hospital in Shreveport, Louisiana, for treatment. Granny was diagnosed as manic-depressive and was twice confined to the Louisiana mental institute at Pineville, where she received electric-shock therapy, a treatment in vogue at the time. At times my mother was almost her old self, and Pa would bring her home to be reunited with us. But her condition didn't stabilize until several years later, when it was discovered that lithium could control it. Fortunately, my mother went on to live a productive and venerated life until her death at ninety-five years old.

Granny's illness couldn't have come at a worse time for my family. A short time after we moved to Dixie, Pa fell eighteen feet off the floor of a drilling rig and landed on his head. The impact fractured two vertebrae in his back. As Pa collapsed forward, he was bent so severely that it burst his stomach. He also broke his big toe, which slammed into the ground as he doubled up. Telling us about it later, Pa said with a wry smile, "I've heard of people getting hit on the head hard enough to break both ankles—but not their big toe."

The vertebrae in Pa's back were fused with bone from his hip; his stomach and big toe were repaired. But he was in a neck-to-hip, heavy plaster-of-Paris cast for two years; a round opening had been left only over his injured stomach.

As always, Pa met the situation in his own laid-back manner. Jimmy Frank and Harold were in college at Louisiana State University in Baton Rouge at the time. They were sharing a GI Bill payment of $110 a month and supplementing their income by Harold's work at the Hatcher Hall cafeteria and Jimmy Frank's work on the LSU horse-and-sheep unit experimental farm. They wanted to drop out of school and come home to work to help support the family, but my daddy insisted they stay in school, remarking dryly over the phone, "We'll make it."

And we did—but not without hardship.

Pa's disability payment from the state was thirty-five dollars a week. In the late 1950s, that money went a little further than it does today, but not nearly far enough. Somehow my family coped. With our mother sometimes away in the hospital, Pa was often left on his own, with five children under his care. He was almost immobile at first, but within a few months, he was able to get around and help with the cooking.

My sister Judy was a rock and did much of the cooking, though all of us helped, and she saw that Silas and Jan got off to school in good order. Fortunately, the school bus stopped in front of our house.

To help make ends meet, Tommy and I gathered pecans and sold them for thirty-five cents a pound. In three hours, we could gather about a hundred pounds—equaling the weekly disability payment. Tommy also cleaned the church building each week in Blanchard, Louisiana, where we worshipped, for five dollars a week. With this money he was able to pay for our school meals, which were fifteen cents per day per child, thanks to Louisiana's liberal school-lunch supplement.

Our food staples became rice and beans, which we bought by the hundred-pound sack. To this we added corn bread. Our meager diet made fresh game and fish doubly appreciated. Fortunately, vegetables were cheap in a farming area, and we purchased what we could with our scanty means from the Biondos, an Italian family that had a commercial truck farm a few miles down the road.

As I noted earlier, a real man can't survive without meat, so it was up to Tommy and me to find some. It wasn't easy, because we no longer had acres and acres of bountiful land surrounding our home. There were plenty of farms around us, but the farmers in the area didn't want anyone on their land. They depended on it for their living and were diligent in warning off what they considered intruders.

Tommy, Silas, and I often led the farmers on wild-goose chases through the woods surrounding their plowed land. When the ground was wet, the red clay in the plowed fields would cling to our shoes and build up to several inches in depth and pounds in weight. My only remedy was to stop occasionally, shake my leg vigorously to dislodge the mud, do the same with my other leg, and then continue on. Progression across the thick land was sometimes nothing more than three steps and a kick!

We never considered what we were doing as poaching on someone else's land. We had our own code. We didn't bother any equipment, crops, or anything on someone else's farm. And I was always careful not to step on any young cotton or corn plants. But if it flew, grew wild, swam, or lived in trees, I figured that it belonged to whoever captured or gathered it. I might have even picked up a ripe watermelon (there were thousands of them out there) every once in a while—wouldn't have wanted it to be overlooked and get overripe!

I can still remember my first encounter with a game warden. I was squirrel-hunting out of season—my family had to eat—and

I had a mess of them. It happened before I repented and was one of the reasons I needed to repent. When I squirrel-hunted, I carried a big, metal safety pin, and I sharpened its end so it would run through the squirrels' legs right above the joint. If I saw a game warden, I'd drop the squirrels, close up the pin, and then take off running like the wind. On this occasion, I was wearing two pairs of old men's argyle socks without any shoes and had my pant legs taped so they wouldn't flop when I was running. I was trying to be as quiet as possible. I was sitting there shooting squirrels when I sensed that someone was watching me. I couldn't see anybody and couldn't hear anybody, but I just had a feeling come over me that I was being stalked in the woods.

> If it flew, grew wild, swam, or lived in trees, I figured that it belonged to whoever captured or gathered it.

Suddenly I heard a stick break behind me, and I turned and saw a man standing there with a gun in his hand. He was wearing a wide-rimmed cowboy hat and identified himself as a game warden. He was standing about twenty yards from me. When I heard the stick break, I dropped the squirrels and they hit the ground.

"Hold it, son," he told me. "I'm a game warden."

"That's what I thought," I said.

I was lean and mean and could run for miles. After the man identified himself as a game warden, I put it into high gear. For the first one hundred yards, he was running with me. But I was grinning and thinking, *This guy doesn't realize that he's not in good enough shape to be running with me.* He was wearing cowboy boots and wasn't properly dressed to keep up with me. A buddy who had dropped me off earlier picked me up on the other side of the woods.

When I was in high school, our basketball coach, Billy Wiggins, asked me if we were killing any squirrels. He said he wanted to go hunting with me, as long as we weren't hunting on land that had been posted for no trespassing. "Of course not," I told him. "You'll be fine."

Coach Wiggins and I went hunting right after daylight one morning, and it wasn't long before I heard a truck coming at a pretty good rate of speed. It was coming across a pecan orchard right toward us. The last two words Coach Wiggins heard were, "Run, Coach!" I took off running in the other direction.

Moving to Dixie also introduced me to frog gigging. Some of the larger bullfrogs have legs bigger than chicken drumsticks and are delicious! We never ate frogs before moving to Dixie, but they were so abundant in the area that they eventually became part of our regular diet. In springtime, in less than an hour we could gather up a large enough bunch to make a meal, even for a family as big as ours. The slough behind our house was overrun with frogs, as were many others just a short distance across the road.

To catch them, we waited until dark and immobilized them by blinding them on the shoreline with a bright flashlight. One of us held the light and another used a long-handled, spring-loaded clamp, or "grab," to "gig" the frog. Some people called the clamps gigs—but the actual sharp-pronged gigs were illegal. The trick was to hit the frog sharply on the back, thus springing the grab and causing it to clamp around the frog, then to lift it out of the water or off the ground quickly so it couldn't use its powerful legs to leap free.

During one particularly memorable frog gigging, we caught a tow sack full of the big ones, probably thirty or forty pounds of them—so many that cleaning them was going to be a chore and take a while. So we laid the sack on the floor by the door when we went into the kitchen for a snack before beginning—carelessly leaving the top only loosely twisted to keep the frogs secure.

While we lingered in the kitchen, the frogs worked themselves out of the bag. When we returned, the bullfrogs were everywhere: leaping and jumping under the beds, tables, chairs, and chest of drawers. They were even inside our shoes—and every other place they could find to hide! One big one was in the middle of a bed!

It took us longer to find and catch the frogs the second time than it had the first. We were still finding them hours later, and when we finally went to bed, we nervously wondered if we would wake up with a cold, clammy companion.

Of course, we grew up with guns in the house. It was the era of Gene Autry and Roy Rogers. Cap pistols were always a big Christmas item in our house, and as we grew older, BB guns became our prized possessions. Shotguns and .22s for each of us were beyond my father's means, but there was always ammunition for his shotgun, and he freely allowed all my brothers and me to use it.

Every one of us learned to shoot with our father's Browning semiautomatic sixteen-gauge shotgun. We also used a Remington .22 that belonged to our uncle Al Robertson and somehow wound up in our house. It was a bolt-action with a seven-shot clip.

From the time Pa purchased his shotgun, the year after World War II ended, he or one of us boys hunted with it almost daily. It would be difficult to calculate how many shells were fired through the old gun's barrel—or the pounds of meat that were downed for our dinner table. Pa bought an entire case of shotgun shells at the beginning of each duck season—and purchased more if that wasn't enough.

The shotgun, more than sixty years old, has been retired. Silas, the last to use it regularly, still has it but doesn't shoot it. Before his death, Pa sent the gun to Browning for refurbishing and repair but received a letter back from the company saying it was "extremely abused." To repair and replace all the worn and damaged components would have cost almost as much as a new one. One of the faults, said the letter, was that the "barrel was kinked and unsafe" and would have to be replaced. Pa had always prized the hard-hitting, close pattern of shot the full-choke barrel delivered (you had to be pretty good to hit with it, as the tight cluster of shot left little room for error). He reluctantly laid the gun aside and bought a new one when times improved.

My brothers and I were all excellent marksmen. Yet my first remembered experience with guns was anything but auspicious. Tommy and I received new BB guns for Christmas one year, but one of them didn't survive. There's still some confusion as to exactly what happened. As my brother Jimmy Frank remembers it, he found Tommy and me fishing in the outhouse toilet hole with straightened wire coat hangers. One of us had been holding a BB gun over the toilet hole. I remember it being Tommy; he, of course, says it was me. Whoever was the culprit was trying to get the other to do something (what isn't remembered) and was bluffing that he would drop the BB gun if he didn't do it. Then he did drop it—accidentally. It disappeared into the mess below.

Tommy remembers that it was his gun and that I did the dropping. Harold remembers that it was his BB gun that was dropped into the hole, and he blames both Tommy and me. I don't exactly recall what happened. Regardless, the gun was never recovered—although desultory fishing operations went on for some time.

When Pa's cast was finally removed, Barnwell Drilling Company put him back to work doing light duty as a tool pusher. He recovered almost completely, and later, after I left to go to college at Louisiana Tech, he and Granny moved south of Baton Rouge to Gonzales, Louisiana, where Pa worked as a pipe fitter in the area's refinery and petrochemical construction boom along the Mississippi River.

Fortuitously, Pa had acquired a union card during the construction of a plant in Marshall, Texas, where he worked for a few months shortly after the war. The plant was under a construction deadline and was hiring anyone who could fit pipe together—particularly those in the drilling industry. Workers were required to obtain a union membership, and it was this reinstated pipe-fitter card from the late 1940s that later gave him the seniority to get high-paying construction jobs—if he was willing to travel to them, which he was in his later years. He worked at a particularly well-paying job in Page, Arizona, in the 1970s, where a coal-fired electricity-generating plant was being built.

Even after we left the log cabin where I grew up and the beautiful woods and swamps surrounding it, I was never far from nature. I always found a way to get back to God's most beautiful creation. Since I was a little kid, I've had this profound connection with and love for deep, dark, unmolested woods. I've always had a longing to be in the deep woods or on the water. I want to be on the lakes, streams, and rivers and be surrounded by everything that comes with it—the ducks, birds, fish, and other wildlife. I guess it's in my DNA, and

> I've always had a longing to be in the deep woods or on the water.

I just love being out there. Even to this day, it's where I want to be. I think part of it is that there's no clutter out there—there are no computers or cell phones (at least not in my duck blind), and constantly updated information isn't being thrown at you from all directions. You might hear a train in the distance every once in a while or see an airplane in the sky flying to New York or someplace else, but your sense of peace and serenity isn't disturbed by clutter.

I have a deep connection with what God created, and what I would love to see more than anything else is a pristine Earth, just like the one He created. There would be no power lines, skyscrapers, or concrete, but there would still be a big ol' kitchen for Miss Kay to make her home-cooked meals. Heaven to me is endless cypress swamps and hardwood forests loaded with game and ducks and not a game warden around! Now, that would be a sight!

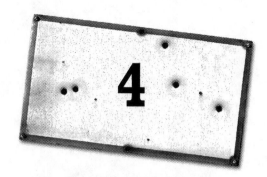

# STRANGE CREATURES

*Rule No. 4 for Living Happy, Happy, Happy*
Don't Try to Figure Out Women (They're Strange Creatures)

I've been on this earth for sixty-six years, and I've reached a conclusion and it's a fact: women are strange creatures. One day I went into the bedroom to go to sleep and then woke up a couple of hours later with my wife, Kay, standing over me.

"Phil, do you love me?" she asked.

"Yeah, of course I do," I said.

"Well, write it down then," she said.

"What?" I asked her as I closed my eyes to go back to sleep.

"Write it down," she said.

I turned over and went back to sleep. I woke up about four A.M. the next morning to go duck-hunting. When I looked at my chair in the living room, I saw a piece of paper with a felt pen sitting right in the middle of it. Then I remembered my conversation with Kay the night before.

I took the sheet of paper and wrote the following: "Miss Kay: I love you. I always have, and I always will."

I told Kay I loved her when she asked me, but she wanted it in writing. You know what Kay did with that piece of paper? She taped it to the headboard of our bed, where it has been for the last few years. I guess she goes to bed every night with the comfort of knowing that I really do love her. Therefore I concluded that women are very strange creatures; there's simply no other explanation for the way they sometimes act.

Miss Kay was the perfect woman for me. I was sixteen and she was fifteen when we were married. Nowadays some people might frown on people getting married that young, but I knew that if you married a woman when she was fifteen, she would pluck your ducks. If you waited until she was twenty, she would only pick your pockets. Now, that's a joke, and a lot of people seem to laugh at it, but there is a certain amount of truth in it.

> I was sixteen and Kay was fifteen when we were married.

If you can find a nice, pretty country girl who can cook and carries her Bible, now, there's a woman. She might even be ugly, but if she cooks squirrels and dumplings, then that's the woman you go after.

I counsel young men all the time, and I tell them to find a woman and eat six of her home-cooked meals before signing on the dotted line. If you're going to spend the rest of your life with her, you at least have to know what the grub is going to taste like. If her cooking passes the test, then she's passed the first level. Even more important, she has to carry a Bible and live by it, because that means she'll stay with you. She also needs to pick your ducks. Some of the young bucks call and ask me, "Hey, what about two out of three?" I tell them two out of three is better than nothing.

As it says in 1 Peter 3:1–6:

> *Wives, in the same way submit yourselves to your own husbands so that, if any of them do not believe the word, they may be won over without words by the behavior of their wives, when they see the purity and reverence of your lives. Your beauty should not come from outward adornment, such as elaborate hairstyles and the wearing of gold jewelry or fine clothes. Rather, it should be that of your inner self, the unfading beauty of a gentle and quiet spirit, which is of great worth in God's sight. For this is the way the holy women of the past who put their hope in God used to adorn themselves. They submitted themselves to their own husbands, like Sarah, who obeyed Abraham and called him her lord. You are her daughters if you do what is right and do not give way to fear.*

That's Miss Kay in a nutshell—she's a kind and gentle woman. In my eyes, she's the most beautiful woman on Earth, on the inside and the outside. She has a natural beauty about her and doesn't need a lot of makeup or fancy clothes to show it. The more makeup a woman wears, the more she's trying to hide; makeup can hide a lot of evil. I think Miss Kay is probably a lot like Sarah was. For some reason, we always talk about Abraham, the father of our faith, but nobody ever mentions Sarah, the mother of our faith. I'm beginning to suspect the reason the mother of our faith is never mentioned is because people don't appreciate a woman who is beautiful on the inside, who is quiet, gentle, and submissive. But God says that being a woman like that is of great worth in His eyes. I believe that Sarah, the mother of our faith, should be revered as much as Abraham, the father of our faith.

Kay and I always were the perfect match. I was our high school quarterback, and she was a cheerleader. We first started going together when she was in the ninth grade and I was in the tenth. One of Kay's older friends decided we might make a cute couple, so she told Kay that I wanted her to walk me off the football field after one of our games. Then the girl came to me and said, "You know that little cheerleader Kay Carroway? She wants you to walk with her off the field after the game." The rest is history, as they say.

Kay and I started dating shortly thereafter, but it didn't last very long. As soon as the Christmas holidays were over, hunting season started, and I was determined to spend all my free time in the woods. I didn't have time for a girlfriend, and I certainly wasn't going to take Kay in the woods with me. Women are a lot like ducks—they don't like mud on their butts. I figured she would just get in the way. But then the next May, Kay's daddy died of a massive heart attack. She was only fourteen at the time, and I knew it was going to be really hard on her. I went to her daddy's funeral, and we made eye contact. I asked her out a few weeks later, and we've been together ever since.

Kay's mother wasn't thrilled when we started dating again. She told Kay, "You don't want to marry into that bunch." But Kay told her mother that even though my family didn't have much money, we loved each other and that was worth a lot more than new cars and fancy clothes.

> Women are a lot like ducks—they don't like mud on their butts.

"They might be poor, but they don't know they're poor," Kay told her mother. "They're a very happy family and love each other. They don't realize they're missing things other people have."

After Kay's daddy died, her mother started dating again and spent a lot of time away from home. Her mother started drinking heavily and became an alcoholic. It was a hard time for Kay, but she always had a safe place to go at our house. Kay is a person of strong principles—many of them learned from her grandmother, whom she called Nannie. Kay spent a lot of time during her growing-up years with Nannie, as both her parents worked full-time in the Ida general store, which was founded by her grandfather and had been in the Carroway family for seventy-five years.

Kay's father worked in the store every day, while her mama tried to do it all: cooking, taking care of the house, and working alongside her husband.

Kay learned how to cook from her grandmother, and I love the woman for teaching her. Kay can prepare anything from wild game to unbelievably good pies, biscuits, and just about anything you can name. The table she sets is renowned among our family, friends, employees, television crewmen, hunters, and others, and there always seems to be a large number of people eating at our house. For years Kay prepared a big meal at the noon hour for anywhere from six to fifteen or more people. She jokes that we could have built ten mansions with the money we've spent feeding everybody over the years. But we don't regret it one bit, and she's enjoyed doing it every day. As it says in Romans 12:13: "Share with the Lord's people who are in need. Practice hospitality."

Because both of her parents worked, Kay spent many childhood hours alone. She filled them with activities like taking in stray cats and other animals. Some of the cats were wild, and she would give them milk and tame them. Her father had bird dogs, and she made friends with them. Her family also had chickens, turkeys, canaries, turtles, baby alligators, and a pony. She likes to joke that she had her own circus while growing up, but she didn't know she was going to marry into one!

Kay's father hunted and fished, and she always loved those

things about him. When I came along with the same attributes, she was naturally drawn to me. Her love for animals also came into play in our relationship. We were soul mates from the very beginning.

It wasn't long before I started taking her with me on fishing or hunting expeditions. My qualms about taking Kay into the woods were quickly relieved. And Kay wasn't only a spectator. She helped catch baitfish, gather worms, hook them onto trotlines, and of course, pick ducks by plucking their feathers to prepare them for cooking. You know you have a good woman when you return home from a hunt and she's standing on the front porch, yelling, "Did y'all get anything?" Before I repented, Kay also drove my getaway car when I was hunting out of season. I always knew my woman was waiting for me on the other side of the woods if I got into trouble.

> Before I repented, Kay also drove my getaway car when I was hunting out of season.

When I received a football scholarship to Louisiana Tech, we moved to Ruston and rented an apartment in the same complex as my brother Tommy, who had received a scholarship to play for the Bulldogs two years earlier. Tommy and his wife, the former Nancy Dennig (they were also high school sweethearts), had been living there for more than a year. With their company, the transition to Louisiana Tech was much easier for us. Kay had not yet graduated from high school, so she finished her senior year at Ruston High School. She was pregnant with our first son, Alan.

We lived in the Vetville Apartments, which the school built in 1945 to accommodate married veterans coming home from World War II. The red-brick apartments were located on south campus, about a mile from the main campus. For Tommy and me, it was like reviving old times. Tommy bought a boat, and I bought a motor for it. We began fishing and hunting in the area waters and woods: the upper Ouachita River and Bayou D'Arbonne Lake, a recently impounded reservoir just north of town. We would usually take someone fishing with us and come home with the daily limit. Kay and Nancy carried a black iron skillet between our apartments until the grease burned it from frying so much fish and other game.

Tommy and I even arranged our schedules so he went to class on Mondays, Wednesdays, and Fridays, and I went on Tuesdays and Thursdays. Tommy would fish while I was in class, and I fished when he was at school. It didn't take me very long to figure out that a few of my instructors loved crappie, or white perch, as they're called in Louisiana. A judicious gift of fresh, filleted white perch to certain instructors, particularly in subjects where I was having difficulty, greatly improved my grades.

One particular class in sports medicine—which was about

taping ankles, diminishing the effects of bumps and bruises, and such—held little interest for me. It was primarily for athletes who were planning to become coaches, which I wasn't sure I wanted to do. Those white perch allowed me to make a passing grade in the course without even attending classes. For whatever reason, the instructor only gave me a C. I thought those fish were worth at least a B. Shoot! Maybe even an A—all those fish!

Generally, I was a quick enough study that I didn't have difficulties in many classes. I basically looked for a strong C average, and I made sure I maintained it. I paid attention in class and took good notes—when I was there. Occasionally, I had to buckle down with a book to get past some difficulty, but I only spent about 30 percent of my time on college. To get better than a C average would have taken too much time and would have interfered with my hunting.

Word quickly spread around campus that I had fish. Even a prominent former Louisiana legislator, who wanted to help me while I was in school, was one of my clients. When the politician paid me, he insisted that he was not buying the fish (selling game fish in Louisiana is illegal) but only paying for me to clean and dress them—to which I readily agreed.

Not everyone on campus was fond of my hobbies. After football practice one day, one of my coaches informed me that the dean of men wanted to see me. I wasn't sure what I had done wrong, but I knew they had me on something. I walked into his office, and he asked me to close the door.

"We have a problem," he said. "Do you know what street you live on? Do you know the name of it?"

"Vetville?" I asked him.

"Let me refresh your memory," he said. "You live on Scholar Drive."

Apparently, the president of Louisiana Tech had given members of the board of trustees a tour of campus the day before.

"When he went to where you live, it wasn't very scholarly," the dean told me. "There were old boats, motors, duck decoys, and fishnets littering your front yard. He was embarrassed. This is an institution of higher learning."

"That's my equipment," I told him.

"But everybody's yard is mowed—except yours," he replied.

"At least the frost will get it," I said. "It will lay down flat as a pancake when the frost gets it."

"It's July," the dean said. "Cut your grass."

One summer the Louisiana Tech football coaches got me a job in Lincoln, Nebraska, as a tester on a pipeline that was being built. Kay loved it and thought it was the biggest adventure of her life, but I missed being in the woods and lakes back home. I could hardly stand it. We only had a company car, which I drove to work, and we lived in a tiny apartment and didn't have a TV, so

## Strange Creatures

Kay woke up every morning and walked miles and miles all over town. I feared Kay was about to die of boredom, so I brought her a little white kitten I found in a cornfield. We named it Snowball, and it was a lot of company for her. When we flew back to Louisiana at the end of the summer, we hid Snowball in a basket packed with sandwiches and travel necessities that we carried on the plane. That cat stayed with us in Louisiana for the next several years and became the first of her many pets.

By then, my interest in playing football was really beginning to wane. My game plan was to hunt and fish full-time and get a college education while doing it—putting as little effort into school as possible. The reason I went into education (I wound up getting bachelor's and master's degrees in education, with a concentration in English) is because you have the summers off, as well as Christmas and Thanksgiving holidays. Consequently, I would have more time to hunt and fish. The only reason I wanted a college degree was so that when people thought I was dumb, I could whip out the sheepskins. Unfortunately, Louisiana Tech didn't offer a degree in ducks.

Unfortunately, Louisiana Tech didn't offer a degree in ducks.

My interest in football was secondary to ducks, but it was paying for my education. I remember riding on a bus going to ball games and scoping out the woods we passed as to hunting possibilities. I just didn't have my mind on football. As a result, I had a checkered playing career. In spite of my God-given talent, I was never fully devoted to the game. Even in junior high, it was merely a social event. When I was playing defensive halfback, I would lightheartedly wave to people in the crowd and grin at things shouted.

I had in my mind that football was a game, something you did solely for entertainment. You go out there and win or lose, but it's certainly not life or death. If you did well, you won. If you didn't do too well, you didn't win. But as far as making a career of football, that never entered my mind—I didn't see the worth of it. I couldn't make much sense out of making a living from work that entailed large, violent men chasing me around—men who are paid for one reason: to run me down and stomp me into the dirt. I just didn't see it.

Despite football not being my primary interest, I still had a decent career at Louisiana Tech. I played quarterback for the Bulldogs from 1965 to 1967 and was the starter in 1966, throwing for more than three hundred yards against Southeastern Louisiana University. During preseason camp the next year, I looked up and saw a flock of geese flying over the practice field and thought to myself, "What am I doing out here?" I walked off the practice field and never went back.

The coaches came to my apartment the next morning and found me cleaning a deer in my kitchen.

"It ain't season," I told them. "I had to bring the meat inside."

No matter how hard they tried, the coaches couldn't persuade me to come back. The quarterback behind me on the depth chart was a guy named Terry Bradshaw, who was a lot more serious about football than I was. Terry started the next three seasons at Louisiana Tech and was the number one pick in the 1970 NFL draft. He became the first quarterback to win four Super Bowl championships, with the Pittsburgh Steelers, and was selected to the Pro Football Hall of Fame. I still tell Terry that if I had never left, he wouldn't have won four Super Bowl rings.

> The quarterback behind me on the depth chart was a guy named Terry Bradshaw.

After I graduated from college, former Louisiana Tech running back Robert Brunet, who was playing in the National Football League, encouraged me to come to Washington, DC, and try out for his team, the Washington Redskins. Vince Lombardi had just been hired as coach.

"You won't beat out Sonny Jurgensen," he told me. "But they've got this hot-dog rookie coming up, Joe Theismann. Robertson, you can beat him hands down. No problem. You make the team, they'll pay you sixty thousand dollars a year."

Some people might think that was pretty good money in the 1960s, but it sure seemed like a pretty stressful way to make a living. I told Brunet, "I don't know—you're up there in Washington, DC, and you miss duck season every year. Do you think I'd stay?" He took a long look at me and said, "Nah, you wouldn't stay."

As far as I was concerned, my football career was over. And as it turned out, my career choice of chasing ducks and whatnot turned out to be a pretty good one. Besides, at the time, I had a young wife and a baby boy. I had their future to worry about, too.

I didn't know I was about to find out how good of a woman my wife really was.

# WHO'S A MAN?

*Rule No. 5 for Living Happy, Happy, Happy*
Always Wear Shoes (Your Feet Will Feel Better)

ccording to the Guinness book of world records, a police constable in India set a world record last year by running 150 kilometers (93.2 miles) in twenty-four hours in his bare feet. A couple of years earlier, a forty-one-year-old man in Oregon ran 102.6 miles barefoot on a rubberized track in less than one day. I'm not sure why Guinness World Records doesn't recognize his *feat* as the record—it seems to me the guy who ran farthest would be the record holder, but what do I know?

While I might not be Zola Budd or a world-record holder, I know neither of those cats have anything on me. When I was about twenty-five or twenty-six years old, I chose to go shoeless for about two years. I simply didn't put any shoes on my feet day after day after day. Here's what I found out: if you don't wear

65

shoes for about two years, you develop pads on the bottom of your feet made of about a half inch of solid, thick, tough callus. You wouldn't believe how tough a man's feet can get! You can literally walk on hot coals—or briars, hot pavement, cold ground in winter—without any shoes. I went duck-hunting with no shoes at all—no waders and no hip boots—just walked out into the water like it was summertime.

We'd go duck-hunting in mid-January, and everybody would be covered up with clothes, but I would be barefoot. We would take people on guided hunts, and one of them would look down and say, "Good grief! This cat doesn't have any shoes on!" I went like it was a summer's day, even if it was only thirty-five degrees outside. I guess you condition your mind and train yourself to be oblivious to pain. On many nights, Miss Kay would have to remove embedded thorns from my feet with a long needle and magnifying glass. Of course, my hunting buddies and I were drinking whiskey straight out of the bottle, so that probably numbed the pain.

After I gave up football at Louisiana Tech, I started running with a pretty rough crowd. It was during the turbulent 1960s, when people my age questioned everything about the government and society in general. The Vietnam War was raging, and I wasn't sure why my brother Si had been sent to Southeast Asia to fight in some country we'd never heard of. It was an era of disillusionment. The status quo and old ways of doing things were being scrutinized with a jaundiced eye. Buttons proclaiming, "Don't trust anyone over thirty"—and a lot worse—were being worn in colleges and elsewhere nationwide.

I listened to the protest songs of Bob Dylan; John Lennon; Peter, Paul, and Mary; the Byrds; and others, and owned a number of their recordings. Clint Eastwood's rebel roles on the screen appealed strongly to me. Years later, when we started making our hunting movies, some of the Eastwood phrases and gritty realism still resonated with me. We had parties and everybody got drunk except for Kay, who wanted nothing to do with the tomfoolery. It went on from when I was about twenty-one or twenty-two until I was about twenty-eight. We got drunk on anything we could get our hands on—running wild and duck-hunting.

> Everybody got drunk except for Kay, who wanted nothing to do with the tomfoolery.

It wasn't just beer and whiskey, either. It was the 1960s, and so usually there was a little marijuana around. We never bought any, but we'd smoke it if it was available. So between the whiskey, diet pills, and various kinds of black mollies (or medicinal speed), we were staying pretty messed up. As far as alcohol, it was mostly confined to whiskey, beer, and wine. Throw in a little marijuana and pep pills, and that was the drug scene, as far as I was concerned. I never got into any of that serious stuff like LSD or heroin; I thought it would have been insanity to stick a needle in my arm. But we pretty well stayed ripped for seven or eight years.

In a lot of ways, I was withdrawing from mainstream society. I was trying to drop back about two centuries to become an eighteenth-century man who relied on hunting and fishing for his livelihood. But I was living in the twentieth century, and everything was constantly changing around me. Hunting and fishing was no longer a way to provide food for my family's table; it was a competition between my buddies and me, and all the rules and laws regulating it were thrown out the window.

Our mantra, or battle cry, was "Who's winning? Who's a man?" We were romping and stomping! We were getting drunk, shooting way too many ducks, and catching too many fish. We were outlaws. It was all about who could kill the most ducks and catch the most fish. We didn't care about anything else.

After leaving college, I took a teaching job in Junction City, Arkansas. The guy who hired me, Al Bolen, persuaded me to take the job with what he called "fringe benefits." One night when I was at home blowing on a duck call, Bolen showed up.

"The fringe benefits are these," Bolen said as he handed me a stack of pictures of ducks and fish.

We agreed on my taking a job teaching tenth-grade English

# Who's a Man?

and physical education to junior-high boys. As soon as I accepted the job, Bolen said, "Let's go get a beer." Before too long, one beer turned into a six-pack, and we became close drinking buddies. And after he showed me the game-rich Ouachita River bottom in the Junction City area, I thought, *Boy, good times are here.*

It was a riotous time. I totaled three new trucks by turning them over or running into trees. It took a good truck to go hunting because we were going into some of the most inaccessible areas of the river bottom. The winch on the front of a truck was forced into use on virtually every trip, as our truck would sink into mud holes on the rutted tracks that passed for roads. The truck would sink so deep that mud flowed onto the floorboards when the doors were opened. When we were stuck, we would stretch out the winch cable, tie it around a tree, pull ourselves back to solid ground, and continue on. It was careless, rollicking, and sometimes very dangerous.

One time, I was running a boat through a small creek with the throttle wide open. Big Al Bolen was in the front of the boat. We were jumping up wood ducks and shooting 'em, which is illegal. But that's what we were doing; we had no fear of the law. When I came around a curve, I was almost on top of a huge pin oak tree that had slid down into the creek. The bank had caved in. There was no time to stop or guide the racing boat around the

69

tree in the narrow confines of the creek. After throttling down for a split second, I decided our best chance was to run up the trunk and sail over the treetop like Evel Knievel. So I gunned the motor.

We hit the trunk, and our boat went airborne, bouncing about three times across the limbs. It came to rest nestled in the limbs, still upright, at about a twenty-five-degree angle. We were two-thirds the way up the tree, leaving Al and me suspended twenty feet in the air above the water—the motor still running.

To get down, we selectively shot limbs off the tree, allowing the boat to slide down far enough so we could pull it back into the creek. I just fired up the motor again, and we were on our way. Big Al reached in his coat and took a swig of whiskey. We continued along, feeling no pain.

On another occasion, when I was trying to save time, I decided to run my aluminum boat up on the bank instead of going through the trouble of pulling it up to the boat ramp, backing the truck and trailer into the water, and loading the boat the usual way. Unfortunately, hidden behind a wall of reeds on the shore was a stump that I hit at full speed, head-on, throwing my passenger in the front of the boat over the stump and out onto the bank.

When the guy was thrown, his legs, which had been under the small front deck of the prow, slid under the deck and hit it with enough force to pop out the rivets that were holding the deck to the side of the boat. His momentum just peeled the deck forward. That probably saved him from breaking his legs. But it ripped the skin off his shins, and his legs immediately turned purple and puffed up. His injuries were severe but didn't incapacitate him. I was thrown from the back of the fourteen-foot boat to the completely crumpled front, breaking a finger. He sailed over the stump, hit the ground, and bounced twice. I was shook up from the collision, and he was pretty

Hidden behind a wall of reeds on the shore was a stump that I hit at full speed.

addled. When he got up, he took off running toward the lake, dove in, and started swimming away from shore. When he was several yards away, he grabbed on to a tree.

I could see he was confused, so I hollered, "What are you doing?"

"I'm trying to get away from that bad thing on the bank!" he replied.

There were a lot of other unforgettable incidents. Once, Silas and I took several men on a guided hunt. I had already taken a bigger boat with some of the hunters to the blind. Si was loading the rest of the men into a smaller, twelve-foot boat. When the four men, whom Si estimated weighed at least 250 pounds each, stepped into the boat, it sank deeper into the water—alarmingly deep! The five men in that overloaded boat pushed it down to the point where the water almost overlapped the sides. But Si persevered and was almost to the blind when (maybe he was traveling a little too fast) the front of the boat dipped and started under.

Si knew the water was not deep in front of the blind and had the presence of mind to grab all the shotguns as the boat completely submerged, dumping everyone into the water. The four guests, who had no idea how deep the water was, thought they were in danger of drowning in their heavy hunting clothes and started floundering and flailing at the water.

Me and the other hunters in the blind realized they weren't in danger and started shouting, "Stand up! Stand up!" Si, holding their saved shotguns, stood neck-deep in water watching them.

Each of the Benelli and Browning shotguns I have owned has ended up at the bottom of a lake multiple times. Each of the shotguns lost during my wild years was recovered, except one that was flipped out of the boat by a limb. Sometimes, I had to resort to buying a wet suit to recover guns from icy, murky waters. Remarkably, the first shotgun I ever owned somehow survived the madness. I worked as a roughneck for a while, following my father into the offshore drilling business. I gave every one of my checks to my parents because I thought that's what I was supposed to do. But with my last check, I asked Pa if I could buy a new shotgun. I purchased a 1962 Browning Sweet 16 shotgun for $150 and still have it today; sometimes I even shoot with it.

During my outlaw years, much of our duck hunting took

place at Moss Lake, where we had a blind halfway up a remarkable cypress tree that stood on the edge of a circle of water surrounded by other cypresses. My brothers Tommy and Jimmy Frank discovered the hole on a bluebird day when they kept seeing flight after flight of ducks circling the area, dropping down into it, and not coming back up. Pa was also hunting with them that day.

Tommy and Jimmy Frank decided to investigate, although they were having a pretty fair shoot from the floating blind they were in, which was in open water about a quarter mile from where all the other ducks were going. Pa stayed in the blind.

My brothers got in their boat and motored straight at the area until they ran aground on a submerged ridge covered with buck brush. Deciding the day was warm enough, although the water was ice-cold, they tied the boat and started wading. They were without waders and just in their hunting boots, but this was the way we hunted back then.

The water was only about knee-deep on the ridge, but then quickly dropped off and rose almost to their waists as they progressed toward where the ducks were still spiraling down. They were soon among the trees and witnessed an amazing sight. It was like something out of primeval times. There must have been five thousand ducks in the opening, probably only thirty yards wide, surrounded by the trees! The entire surface of the open water was completely covered with ducks—so many that they crowded shoulder-to-shoulder, like a giant raft made of ducks. It was a year when the male-female ratio was out of balance, and most were mallard drakes, their green heads standing out sharply in the dark mass. Ducks continued to spiral down from above as my brothers watched in amazement.

Jimmy Frank got tangled in a dead tree underneath the water, but Tommy kept moving forward. The ducks spotted him. They stirred but didn't fly. When he felt he was close enough, Tommy shot them on the water, surprisingly downing only two ducks. Still the ducks didn't fly away but continued to mill around, dodging in and out among the trees. And more ducks kept spiraling down from above the hole.

By the time it was over, my brothers downed a total of ten ducks.

As amazing as the number of ducks on the water was, even more impressive was the old cypress. It was nearly twenty feet wide at the base and hollow from water level to about thirty feet up. The opening was wide enough for a man to easily pass through, and it was there that Tommy and I, along with our friend Maurice Greer, built a blind with a porch from which eleven men could shoot.

The big hollow at the water level was so large that a pirogue could be pulled into it (a larger boat was used to reach the area and was hidden some one hundred yards away, beneath some buck brush). After sinking the pirogue to conceal it, we made our way to the blind above by climbing up through the hollow on several boards that we'd nailed on the inside to form a ladder. When we got to the shooting porch, ducks that circled to look at the decoys often flew right in front of us. At times, we actually shot down at the ducks.

The old cypress tree was one of the Almighty's great creations, and it's where we spent many glorious mornings together as a family. But during my rompin' and stompin' days, I never embraced its beauty and rarely cherished the time I spent with my father and brothers.

The only things I seemed to be worried about were how many ducks I could kill and when my next drink was coming.

> The old cypress tree was one of the Almighty's great creations, and it's where we spent many glorious mornings together.

By then, I had a growing family at home. Our sons Jase and Willie had been born, and Kay was at the end of her rope with me. I was always out, partying with my buddies, leaving her alone to raise our three sons. I was growing more distant from everything I had known and been taught and was pulling even farther away from the people who loved me the most. Kay felt her entire life was in ruins and that she had failed as a wife. After a while, the school where I was teaching could no longer ignore my public conduct. Students and their parents were beginning to notice my boorish behavior, and my days as a teacher and coach were numbered.

Sadly, even as my life continued to spiral out of control, like a downed duck falling from the sky, I failed to realize that "callous" also described me as a man.

# HONKY-TONK

*Rule No. 6 for Living Happy, Happy, Happy*
Put the Bottle Down (You'll Thank Me in the Morning)

**A**fter I resigned from my teaching position (before the school board could fire me), I made one of the biggest mistakes of my life: I leased a honky-tonk in the middle of nowhere. I managed the place, worked the bar, cooked for the customers, and broke up occasional fights. One of my specialties was something I called squirrel mulligan: ten pounds of freshly killed squirrels, ten pounds of onions, ten pounds of potatoes, and enough crumbled crackers to give it the proper thickness. It didn't taste too bad, and its aroma smelled better than the overwhelming scent of urine and stale beer that permeated the place. I also served fried chicken, pickled pig's feet, and boiled eggs, though most of the regulars, including me, were only there to drink as much beer and whiskey as we could.

It was a rough, rough place. I managed the place before

integration was firmly established in the South, so my honky-tonk was somewhat unusual. It was really a segregated beer joint, which you didn't see very often. The blacks drove up in the back, and we had their jive going on back there, and the rednecks came through the front. I was in the middle, serving and cooking for everyone, while trying to keep the peace.

Kay and our three sons moved out in the middle of nowhere with me. The bar was a long, low, one-story wood building, unpainted and yellowed. Our trailer home and another building were roughly attached to it, making the whole complex an irregular U-shape. It wasn't very pretty, and it certainly wasn't the proper place to be raising my boys. Kay, of course, worried about me constantly, so she worked as a barmaid most nights to make sure I stayed out of trouble. She never was much of a drinker—probably because she saw what alcohol did to her mother—but she was right beside me on most nights, watching me slowly drink away our lives.

After a while, my parents, brothers, and sisters started to hear what was happening with me. One night, my younger sister, Jan, drove out to the bar with William "Bill" Smith, one of the preachers at White's Ferry Road Church in West Monroe, Louisiana. Jan lived close by in the area, so she knew more than the rest of my family how far I had strayed from my former ways. She was determined to save me and enlisted Bill Smith to help her.

When they walked into the bar, Smith found me sitting at a desk in the connecting structure. I had a quart bottle of beer in my hand.

"You some kind of preacher?" I immediately asked him. When Smith told me he was, I added, "You ever been drunk?"

"Yes, I used to drink a few beers," he told me.

"Well, what's the difference between you and me?" I asked him. "You've been drunk, and I'm getting drunk right now. There ain't a dime's worth of difference between you and me, Jack. You ain't putting any Bible on me. That's the way I was born."

At that moment, one of my patrons stuck his head in the door and said, "Phil, your sister's running into some problems out there in the bar."

> "You some kind of preacher?" I immediately asked him.

Jan was in the barroom handing out religious tracts. The patrons were cussing and carrying on as usual—getting drunk. One guy was arguing with her. "Hey! Hey!" I said as I stepped in.

They all turned around, looking at me. "This is my little sister. She's handing out religious tracts. Let her hand them out. But don't be messing with her, or you're going to deal with me."

"This is your sister?" one of them asked.

"Yes. She's going to do whatever she does here," I told him. "Leave her alone!"

Jan, now in a little bit of a dither, went on handing out tracts—in a dead quiet—until she had given everyone one. I turned around, went back to Smith, and ordered him out of my bar.

As Jan and Smith walked back to their car in the drizzling rain, with the country music wailing behind them in the front of the building and rhythm and blues blaring in the back, he exclaimed, "Whew! I don't think he's ready! Let's give him a little time. I'm glad I got out of there without getting beaten up!"

Although Smith's visit left me unmoved, Kay later began to study the Bible with him. She knew our marriage and lives were rapidly deteriorating.

A few months later, I hit what I thought was rock bottom. One night the couple that owned the bar came in and informed me they were going to raise my rent. So I decided I'd hightail it out of the place after fulfilling the last two months on my lease. An argument ensued, and I ended up throwing the man and woman across the bar, injuring both of them pretty badly. By the time the fight was over, there were four police cars out front. Ambulances were also on the way to take the bar owners to the hospital; I'd whipped both of them pretty good. I went out the back door and jumped in my truck before the police could arrest me. Before I left, I told Kay, "I'm going to the swamps or somewhere. You're not going to see me for a few months."

# Honky-Tonk

Of course I left Kay behind to clean up my mess. The police issued a warrant for my arrest, but Kay persuaded the bar owners to drop criminal charges against me. The plea bargain came with a hefty price: the bar owners took nearly all the money we'd saved while operating the honky-tonk. They wouldn't even let Kay get our personal belongings—a washer and dryer and photographs and keepsakes of our boys—out of a storage shed in back. Fortunately, Kay had hidden about two thousand dollars in a lockbox and used that money to move our trailer—which we were still paying for—back to Louisiana.

After the fight, I got out of Arkansas. Even though Kay paid off the bar owners, I didn't know whether there were still arrest warrants out for me—assault and all that stuff. The bar owners had a restraining order against me, so I couldn't go anywhere near them. I stayed out of Arkansas for about a decade because I didn't know whether they were going to try to get me, put me in jail, or what.

Kay moved our trailer to a spot beside Lake D'Arbonne at Farmerville, Louisiana, as she and I had discussed during a phone conversation. I eventually got a job working in the oil fields offshore in the Gulf of Mexico. In the meantime, Kay had to handle everything concerning the move back to Louisiana. For about the next year, she and I somehow endured, though our marriage was under tremendous strain.

# HAPPY, HAPPY, HAPPY

While I was a fugitive, I kept hunting and fishing as much as I could—sandwiching the activities I loved around my offshore job. The incident at the bar didn't stop me from romping, stomping, and ripping with my drinking buddies. Kay later said I wasn't an alcoholic, only a problem drunk. But it was pretty clear I had a problem. She always held out hope that I would change my ways, and she believed that if we moved to a new location and met new people, things would get better. But they never did; things only got worse.

> Kay said I wasn't an alcoholic, only a problem drunk. But it was pretty clear I had a problem.

One rainy night, Kay came home late from work, and I accused her of running around on me, which I knew she would never do. It was a life-changing event for Kay, and she remembers the details and aftermath of the incident better than I do:

I think Phil's problems really started during our first year at Louisiana Tech. He was playing football but had a wife and baby at home. It was a lot of grown-up responsibility for an eighteen-year-old, and he really wasn't ready for it. He saw his teammates going out and partying all the time, and he wanted to go out, too. I think that's why he so easily got in with the wrong group—he wanted to be like the single guys who had all the freedom. He'd never really experienced the single life since we married so young. I tried to do the party scene with him, but I couldn't leave Alan, who was only a baby. I didn't think it was right. I didn't like drunkenness. I didn't think it was wrong to have a drink, but I just didn't like the whole scene.

I really thought that after Phil graduated from Louisiana Tech and we moved to Junction City, Arkansas, he would settle down. After all, he was going to be a coach and teacher, which came with a lot of responsibility. But Al Bolen, the man who hired him, was as big a party guy as Phil, so the partying and running around only continued.

When Phil leased the bar, people couldn't believe that I went out and stayed with him. I worked as a barmaid, and the people there really respected me and told everybody, "Don't you talk ugly to her. She doesn't drink and she's a nice lady." It surprised me that those people were so protective of me. They always asked me why I was in the bar if I didn't drink, but when I decided to stay with Phil and remain faithful to him, I felt it was my duty to protect him. With me at the bar, I felt he wouldn't get in as much trouble as he would if I wasn't there.

The year after the bar fight was probably the worst time of my life. Phil was working offshore and drinking more than he ever had before. When I came home one night, he accused me of having an affair, which was so stupid. I had never done anything like that, and it wasn't because his friends weren't hitting on me, either. It was because I wasn't that kind of person. I always told him, "If I leave you, I'll divorce you and find somebody else if I want to. I would never cheat on you."

# HAPPY, HAPPY, HAPPY

I've always considered myself a good person. I don't know if it's my personality or what, but I've always been a very serving person. During all of Phil's troubles, I felt like I was operating on my grandmother's faith and what she instilled in me. I finally realized you have to have your own faith. Phil was cursing me and calling me every ugly word under the sun. It was the first time in my life that I felt hopeless. When I was younger, I read that a person can live so long without water, so long without food, but that you can never live without hope. I have always believed that hope and dreams are what keep us going. My entire life, all I had ever wanted was to be the best wife and mother I could. I didn't want riches or fame; I wanted to have a loving, good, and safe home for my boys—that's all.

> "When I came home one night, he accused me of having an affair, which was so stupid."

The night Phil accused me of having an affair, I hit rock bottom. I went to the bathroom and cried. It was the first time in my life that I didn't know how to fix the problem. It's the only time in my life that I had suicidal thoughts. I just wanted to go to sleep and not wake up because I didn't know how to fix our lives and didn't know what to do. Would I have gone through with it? I hope not, but I really wanted Phil to suffer because of what he was doing to me.

But as I sat there contemplating what to do, I heard my little boys' house shoes running down the hall. Alan was nine, Jason was five, and Willie was three. Alan knocked on the bathroom door and said, "Mama, don't be sad. Don't be crying." I'll never forget what he said next: "God's going to take care of us. You'll be all right. We'll be all right. Daddy will quit drinking one day." It was like a light went off in my head. I thought, "Oh, my goodness, what am I thinking? I've got three little boys. Am I going to leave them behind to live with a drunk?" Phil couldn't have taken care of the boys in his condition.

I prayed to God and asked Him to help me find some kind of peace. Obviously, my life wasn't going right, but I knew I had to take care of my three boys. The next day, I was watching a TV show called *Let the Bible Speak,* and there was Bill Smith, the preacher Jan brought up to the beer joint. The things he was saying were what I needed to hear—what I wanted in my life. He was speaking about how to obtain peace and hope. So I called the number on the screen and set up an appointment to meet him the next day. Somebody kept the kids for me, and I went over to White's Ferry Road Church.

One of the first things Bill Smith asked me was, "If you die, do you think you'll go to heaven?" I told him, "I sure do. Let me tell you what I've been living with." I went into how bad Phil was and how I'd still been a faithful and loving wife to him. Smith asked me if I thought I'd earned my way to heaven, and I told him that I certainly had. Smith asked me if I had peace and hope in my life, and I told him, "Now, that's the problem." There was some sort of disconnect because I felt I had earned my way to God, but I didn't have any hope and didn't feel any peace.

Smith shared the gospel with me, and I became convinced that I couldn't be saved on my own good works. I was a good person, but I was a good person without Jesus Christ in my life. That's not enough. Smith told me that if I wanted to, I could leave the church that day with Jesus Christ in my life. I confessed to Jesus and made him the Lord of my life and was baptized. The best thing Smith told me that day was that when I went home, Phil would still be as drunk as ever and would still act terrible. But Smith told me I would be different because I would have God's spirit living in me. He told me that when things were bad here on Earth, I just had to think about my next life in heaven and how wonderful it would be. I left his office as a Christian and started developing my own faith.

I went home and tolerated Phil's behavior because I knew God would help me through it. I was working in the offices at Howard Brothers Discount Stores in West Monroe, and Phil wasn't doing much of anything besides drinking and staying out all night. I came home from work late one night, and Phil started in on me about running around on him again. He looked at me and said, "I'm sick of you. It was bad enough that I had to live with you before, but now you're a holy roller." He also called me a Bible thumper and a goody two-shoes. "You think you're an angel," he said. "I want you to get out and take the three boys with you. I want y'all to leave." He knew he couldn't separate me from my sons.

I asked Phil, "Are we messing up your bachelor's life?" He told me yes, and I knew there was nothing else to do but leave. Our little boys were so sad and had tears streaming down their faces. They didn't want their daddy drunk, but they loved their father. We stayed with Phil's

My parents
James H.
and Merritt
Robertson

My third-grade
picture

Playing baseball in my junior year at
North Caddo High School, Vivian,
Louisiana

During my playing days
conferring with North
Caddo coach Ed Sigrest

The Robertson men in the
early 1970s in Gonzales,
Louisiana. Left to right:
James (Pa), Tommy, Jimmy
Frank, Si, Harold, and me

Kay and me—high
school sweethearts

Kay as a sophomore at
North Caddo

Kay with her Papaw
Carroway and miniature
pony, Tony

My sophomore
year at Louisiana
Tech (1966).
Pictured here
are the backfield
and receivers.
Terry Bradshaw is
number 12 and I
am number 10, on
the back row third
from left.

My first year teaching English
and PE in Junction City,
Arkansas

Alan, Jase, Kay, and me in
1972

From left to right: Alan, Kay,
Willie, and Jase, Christmas
1976

Al Bolen and me in the
early 1970s

Me in front of Granny and Pa's
house in Luna, Louisiana, holding
catfish caught on the Ouachita
River

The boys—left to right: Willie, Jep, and
Jase—waiting on me to return with the
fish

Me at the lathe in the mid-1970s

Still building duck calls in the 1990s

Building duck calls is a family affair.

Me with Peggy Sue out on my land

Mac Owen and me hunting among the cypress trees of Louisiana

Here I am preaching the gospel at a speaking event.

Grand opening of the new location in 2010

The Duckmen accepting our Golden Moose awards in 2010

Si and me enjoying some brother time

Jimmy Frank, Tommy, and I admire the five-hunter
limit from the last hunt of 2011.

brother Harold for one night. He told us we could only stay one night because he was afraid of what Phil would do. I never held that against Harold because I didn't know what Phil would do either.

The boys and I moved into a low-rent apartment, and White's Ferry Road Church helped me pay the rent and get some furniture. We were apart from Phil for about three months; I was really hiding from him. I put everything in my maiden name, thinking he wouldn't be able to find us. I went to lunch every day with one of my girlfriends at work, and one day when we came back to the office, we saw Phil's old, gray truck in the parking lot. Phil's head was lying on the steering wheel, so I figured he'd driven there, then passed out drunk. I told my friend to go on into the office and watch out the window and if she saw Phil flashing a gun to call the police. "You can't go out there by yourself," she told me. "Let's go in and call the police." But I didn't want Phil following me into my office and hurting anybody, so I told her to watch out the window and call the police if anything bad happened.

I walked up to Phil's truck and opened the door. His face rose up, and there were big tears streaming down his face. I had never seen him cry. The macho man never cried. He looked at me and said, "I can't eat. I can't sleep. I can't do anything. I want my family back." He told me he wouldn't drink anymore and was done with partying. Of course, I'd heard that many times before. I felt God's courage inside me and told him, "Phil, you can't do it by yourself, buddy. You just can't." Phil told me he needed help and then asked me where he could find it.

"There's only one person who can help you," I told him.

"God?" Phil asked.

"Yes," I said.

"I don't know how to find Him," Phil replied.

As a boy, Phil had gone to church and Sunday school, but he had been away from God for a long time. I told Phil I knew someone he could talk to and to be back at my office at five thirty, when I got off work. I told him I'd lead him to my apartment. When I went back upstairs to my office, I was so happy I sailed up three steps at a time. I called Bill Smith, the preacher, and told him to be at my apartment at five forty-five. He said, "Well, let me check my calendar."

> "I can't eat. I can't sleep. I can't do anything. I want my family back."

"What is more important than one lost soul coming back to the Lord?" I asked him. "If you have anything else, you have to cancel it."

"You know what?" Smith told me. "Nothing is more important than that."

Smith and his wife, Margaret, met Phil and me at my apartment. The first thing Phil told him was: "I don't trust you." Smith told Phil that he could understand why he didn't trust him. "Considering the people you've been running around with, I wouldn't trust anyone either," Smith told him. Then Smith held up his Bible and said, "Do you trust this?"

"Yeah, I trust that book, but I'm going to check out everything you say," Phil said. "I don't take any man's word for anything."

I went into the back room with the boys and Margaret, and Phil and Smith studied the Bible together for several hours. When they were finished, Phil told Smith he was going to check out everything they'd talked about, and they scheduled another meeting for the next night. We let Phil move into our apartment, and the first thing the boys asked him to do was bring back our big TV. The next day, the boys and I left to go to the grocery store. When we returned home, I found a note from Phil, telling us to come to White's Ferry Road Church. When I walked into the back door of the church, Phil was already in the baptistry. He's so impatient, he couldn't wait for me to get there! Smith had taken Phil's confession and was in the process of baptizing him. I looked down at our boys and they were crying. Alan looked at me and said, "I guess that devil is going to be gone now." Phil was twenty-eight years old, and our lives were starting over.

Once I make a decision, I'm all in and there's no second-guessing. After I was baptized, I attended regular church services three times a week (twice on Sunday). I also studied the Bible with someone or a group the other five nights of the week. I went back to teaching and worked for Ouachita Christian School, which had just opened in Ouachita Parish. I felt like I needed time with Christian people to get me back on my feet spiritually, so I did that for about two years. Because everything was in Kay's maiden name, my old friends couldn't find me. When they finally tracked us down after about three or four months, I told them never to come back. It was about five years after I was baptized before the pull of sin finally stopped.

Although I was healing spiritually and was beginning to earn the trust of my wife and children again, there still seemed to be something missing in my life. It's funny how things work sometimes. Even during my romping, stomping, and ripping days, when I was at my lowest point, the hunting and fishing were actually a training ground for what I wanted to do with the rest of my life. It was in my blood, and I spent as much time as I could doing it. When I was partying, we would go from the beer joint to the woods or lakes and back. Yet out of all that heathen activity came my expertise for duck hunting and catching fish, as well as my dream to one day build my own duck calls. Even as I sank deeper into that wild lifestyle and as my values and sense of worth were severely battered, there was a core of resilience inside that kept me going.

> Out of all that heathen activity came my expertise for duck hunting and catching fish, as well as my dream to one day build my own duck calls.

I wasn't entirely sure where it was going to lead me—until one day Kay found something in the back of a newspaper.

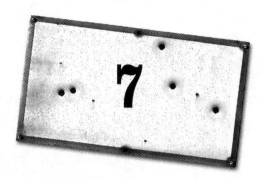

# SPORTSMAN'S PARADISE

*Rule No. 7 for Living Happy, Happy, Happy*
Buy a House Near Water (It's a Lot More Fun)

**W**hen I started my Christian walk, I began a very intensive study of the Bible. Like I said, I don't do anything halfway; it's my personality to become immersed in something once I set my mind to it. I attended services at White's Ferry Road Church at least twice a week and spent the other five days of the week studying God's Word with groups of friends or alone. I was determined to become a scholar of the Bible, to understand the true meaning of every verse of Scripture, so I might one day be able to spread His word to other people who found themselves in the predicament I once struggled through.

After a couple of years, I regained my confidence and had a new outlook on life. But in the back of my mind, I still wanted to return to hunting and fishing, which was always my consuming passion. Kay understood my struggle and was sympathetic when I told her that I could make more money as a commercial fisherman than at my teaching job. It was something I had been thinking about for a few years, as I still yearned to be in the woods, lakes, and rivers, where I was most happy and at peace.

With a lot of faith in me, as always, Kay encouraged me, saying she thought it was a good plan. Together we made a life-changing decision. We decided I would quit my teaching job at Ouachita Christian School and begin fishing. We planned to adopt a lifestyle that would involve virtually living off the land, just like my family had done when I was a child. I told Kay to search for land with water that eventually flowed into the sea. I was gambling that by doing what I wanted to do, I could make a living for my family—which was still growing. Eventually Kay and I would have four sons; Jeptha, our last, was born in 1978.

Kay found six and a half acres of land just off the Ouachita River at the mouth of Cypress Creek outside of West Monroe, Louisiana. It was at the end of a dirt road in one of the most heavily forested areas on the river. The classified advertisement in the newspaper described it as a "Sportsman's Paradise." When we drove out to see the land, I knew it was perfect as soon as we crested the hill that leads down to the house where we still live today. The place was absolutely perfect.

## Sportsman's Paradise

The real estate lady sensed my excitement and told me, "Now, Mr. Robertson, I'm required by law to inform you that this home sits in a floodplain."

"Perfect," I told her. "I wouldn't want it if it didn't."

Our land fronts a small slough, which eventually flows to the sea by way of Cypress Creek and the Ouachita, Red, Atchafalaya, and Mississippi Rivers. When we purchased the property, two houses stood on the land: one a substantial three-bedroom, white frame house, the other a primitive camp house of weathered, green-painted lumber. The latter was subject to being flooded during times of high water when the Ouachita River overflowed its banks. The front yards of both houses sloped gently down to the slough, which wrapped around the land on the north side.

*When we drove out to see the land, I knew it was perfect as soon as we crested the hill.*

Behind the houses, the hill continued steeply upward, making a large promontory that jutted out into the juncture of the river and creek. The land was covered with towering oaks and pines.

The Ouachita River varies from a small, crystal-clear stream flowing over the rugged rocks of the Ouachita Mountains in southwest Arkansas to a muddy, turgid, intermingled flood where it joins the Red River just before emptying into the Mississippi

River in southern Louisiana. Deep woods and substantial wet-lands lie alongside most of its 605-mile length.

*Washita* (another spelling of the river's name) is an Indian word meaning "good hunting grounds." The Ouachita Indians, for whom the river is named, and several other tribes—including the Caddo, Chickasaw, Osage, Tensa, and Choctaw—lived along its banks. I later discovered, from potsherds and other relics I found—including a human skeleton uncovered by a spate of rain—that our land was inhabited in the distant past. A team of archeologists from Northeast Louisiana University in Monroe established that the skeleton I found was very old and that of an Indian. In the past, the promontory had been a thriving Indian encampment. Indians lived there for centuries, sallying out to hunt and fish from the small peninsula whose natural advantages gave them easy access to the teeming wildlife and fishing of the area. When their time passed, the river served as a passage into northern Louisiana and southwestern Arkansas for settlers of the area.

When I saw the site and its location for the first time, I knew instantly that it was the land I wanted. It was where I would launch my career as a commercial fisherman, and it was where I would teach my sons the survival skills I learned from my father during my youth.

Even though the property was relatively cheap, it was out of our price range. Fortunately, my parents were making plans to return to Louisiana from Arizona, and Pa had enough money for a down payment on a small place for retirement. They still owned my boyhood home in Dixie, Louisiana, which they were renting to a poor family that was often behind on the monthly payment. My parents' dilemma was that while they could make a down payment on any retirement home they wanted, they weren't sure how they would maintain it once they grew older.

When I showed them the old Indian settlement, they fell in love with it as much as I had. Granny could sense that it would be an excellent retirement home, and Pa was particularly impressed with its solitude and hunting and fishing opportunities. When we began to explore how to acquire the place, we came up with a way that would fit both families' needs. Kay and I needed a down payment, and Pa and Granny needed to eliminate their worries about monthly payments and long-term maintenance. Having two houses on the place was a godsend that led to an agreement that would solve our problems. Pa and Granny used their savings for the down payment, and Kay and I agreed to make monthly payments and maintain the property. The arrangement led to several years of happy, happy, happy living in a place we all loved.

Pa and Granny elected to live in the camp house, while my larger family took the house farther up the hill. We all settled comfortably into our new homes, and I began my career as a commercial fisherman. Pa and my sons were right alongside me as I started my fishing business. For Pa, it was a return to a way of life close to that of his childhood and my younger years at Aunt Myrtle's farm. At first he actively hunted and fished the bountiful area surrounding our property; then, as he grew older, he gravitated more to taking care of the garden he'd started. Most of our food, from spring to fall, came from Pa's garden. Our meat came from fish we caught or from ducks, squirrels, and deer we shot. We usually ate fish three times a week.

Pa's first garden on the edge of the slough flooded every year or so. The floodwaters enriched the soil but sometimes delayed planting, so he began another level plot farther up the hill, which stayed dry even in the wettest of years. As Pa grew older, however, he began to slow down, and his interests became narrower. He spent his later years close to home, tending the fire in the iron stove that heated their house and playing dominoes and other games with his family and grandchildren. He enjoyed the role of patriarch of his large extended family, which numbered more than sixty during his lifetime, and he even bragged at one point that he was the oldest Robertson of his line left.

Pa helped me with projects around the place, such as building a boat launch and dock, house repairs, and a multitude of tasks that kept the place going. Both families were bent on making our lives successful. It was Granny who suggested a drop box at the boat launch we built, where customers using it could deposit payment of a small fee. The honor system is still in place—the suggested fee is two dollars—and the boat launch is used daily by those launching their boats onto Cypress Creek and the Ouachita River.

Once I began fishing full-time, it didn't take long for the business to become successful. Before too long, I was making more money than I did as a teacher. The fishing was profitable from the beginning and grew as I made enough money to buy more nets and trotlines. I caught about sixty thousand pounds of fish—thirty tons—the first year, and that's about what we averaged annually.

> Before too long, I was making more money fishing than I did as a teacher.

We caught a cascade of catfish, buffalo, gaspergou (freshwater drum), alligator gar, and a number of white perch. The catfish were worth about seventy cents a pound, the buffalo thirty cents, and the market always determined the gar's price. More gar are caught and sold in Louisiana than any other freshwater fish. Fish brings a higher price during cold weather; in warm weather almost everybody in Louisiana fishes, and the surplus catch goes into the commercial market, driving prices down.

The white perch, or crappie, are game fish and cannot be sold. They are lagniappe and usually ended up on our dinner table. The man we sold our fish to at the market ate only the poorer parts of the fish, the parts he couldn't sell. But that wasn't my style. I fed my family the best of my catch and sent the rest to market. My selectivity continues today, as I carefully pick the best of the ducks killed on a hunt, usually teal or wood ducks. If I'm doing all the work, why should someone else enjoy the pick of the litter?

I decided early on that if my boys were going to eat the fish, they were going to help catch them, too. Setting out the nets wasn't too much of a task for me, but getting the fish from my boat, up the hill, and into my truck took some serious work. When it rained, it was even more arduous because the hillside was slick and muddy. After one catch, I was slipping and sliding all over the hill, struggling to carry a heavy tub to my truck.

When I got to the house, the boys were all there. Kay was getting ready to take the fish to town and sell them. We did this about two or three times a week; it was the only money we made. The boys usually went with her and always looked forward to it. I went in the house and said to them, "Y'all come over here and sit down for a few minutes. I want to explain something to you.

"Y'all are fixing to go to the store," I told them. "There will be bubble gum and shopping—y'all are going to have a big ol' time. I want you to realize that all that money you're going to spend is coming off those fish out there. You understand that?"

"Yes, sir," they answered quietly. They knew this talk was serious.

"What I can't figure out is, if you're getting all that money from the fish, why doesn't someone come down there when that boat pulls up and grab the other side of that tub to help me up the hill? That's what I can't figure out."

They all sat there staring at me, like I was speaking Spanish.

"Hey, just a thought," I said. "I can get 'em up the hill. But it would be a lot easier with y'all helping me."

From that day forward, whenever I pulled in with the boat, I'd see the whole little group coming down the hill. They'd have their tubs and be ready to help. It was a lesson that stayed with them. All four of my boys came to realize that the work was a family enterprise, and they needed to pitch in. In fact, the lesson took so well that each of them still works for Duck Commander, as do several other relatives and extended family. If you want a job with our outfit, it helps if you're blood kin.

I also assigned my boys one of the worst jobs that came with commercial fishing: assembling the bait. I would buy a fifty-five-gallon drum of rotten cheese and let it sit until it was covered in maggots. It needed to smell really bad and be as smelly and nasty as possible to draw the catfish to my nets. When the rotten cheese was ready, I'd get my boys up at daylight. They'd reach down into the drum and grab a handful of the mess and stuff it into socks. I know they were gagging the entire time—and I'm sure they lost their breakfast more than a few times—but it was a job that had to be done.

Later, when the boys were in high school, I decided I wanted to get into crawfishing. The problem with crawfish is you can never have enough bait. And crawfish are attracted to bait that's even nastier than what a catfish likes to eat. A crawfish will literally eat anything—as long as it's dead and smells really bad. So when Kay took the boys to town to sell the fish, I always told Alan, Jase, Willie, and Jep to be on the lookout for roadkill. If they spotted a dead possum or raccoon in the road, they'd pick it up and throw it into the back of the truck. They'd bring the dead animals home, chop them up, and then throw them into the crawfish nets.

Of course, I never wanted to waste anything. We had an old deep-freezer in my shop and they threw the excess roadkill in there. By the end of every summer, the freezer was filled with dead cats, dogs, deer, coons, opossums, ducks, and anything else they could find in the road. The freezer smelled so bad it would have been quarantined if health officials ever caught wind of it! My boys also hunted for snakes and put them in the freezer. They baited snake traps in the water with little perch and then pulled the traps in at night. They'd blast the snakes with shotguns, which I'm sure was a lot of fun for them.

# Sportsman's Paradise

The biggest single catch I ever made was on an early morning one June. It came after we decided to launch Duck Commander as a business, so I had recently given up commercial fishing. I was only fishing for fun and to put some fish on the family table. I was using a six-foot hoop net about twenty feet long, with two-inch mesh. My son Jase was fishing with me and I told him, "I'm going to put this old big net out and catch us some Ops."

> By the end of every summer, the freezer was filled with dead cats, dogs, deer, coons, opossums, ducks, and anything else they could find in the road.

"Ops" is short for Opelousas, which are flathead catfish. I think they're the best eating species of all the freshwater commercial fish in Louisiana. Also called the motley, yellow cat, or shovelhead, the flathead catfish is aggressively predacious and known for eating everything in sight. Some of them weigh as much as 120 pounds.

I set the net out on the other side of the river and up from the boat a little bit. I dropped it in about eighteen feet of water with a little current, but not much, just enough to hold the net open. I came back after about three days. I reached and grabbed the rope and started up with the net. I thought, "That thing must be hung!" But it kept coming; it was heavy, heavy!

I kept coming with that heavy net. When I had about three hoops gathered up, I could feel something moving the whole net ever so slightly. When I got the net up high enough to where I could see down into it a little bit, all I could see were blue cats! One look, and I realized there was way more fish than I could get into my boat! It was just too much weight! There were too many fish to even move them!

So I wound up with about two-thirds of my net in the boat and a third of it in the water—literally crammed with blue catfish. After tying off the hoops that I had pulled out of the water, the rest of the net formed a bag that hung straight down from the boat. It was some weight! But the fish were quietly swimming inside the net—I had 'em!

Now I was free floating. I cranked up my motor and let it idle, but I was moving forward—those swimming fish were moving my boat. I came across the river at an angle, going real slow. I made it to the mouth of Cypress Creek and almost home with a catch of biblical proportions. I headed for the bank, where the water depth begins to decrease rapidly. The net started dragging the bottom. When I got close to the bank, I jumped out of the boat and into the water, which was about four or five feet deep. I pulled the boat closer to the bank. The fish came alive in the shallow water and were making a rumble!

I went to my truck, locked its hubs to get it into four-wheel drive, and backed into the water as close as I could get to the boat and the fish. I climbed into the boat and, with a large dip net, started scooping up the thrashing fish and putting them into my washtubs. After throwing about fifty to sixty pounds into a tub, I transferred the fish to my truck. The blue cats weighed from three to twenty pounds each. From the time I started pulling up the net, I toiled with the rascals for more than two hours.

I mean, it was work! I was sweatin'! I filled the truck bed until it was mounded up with fish. Then I drove the truck out of the water onto solid ground. Both Jase and Kay, when they came out and saw those fish, were stunned. Jase said he had never seen so many fish in one pile. When they took them to town to sell, they tipped the scales at one thousand pounds! Kay and Jase came back with three hundred dollars, and they sold them cheap— thirty cents a pound.

That's the most fish I ever caught in one net. Another time I caught eighteen Opelousas cats in one net weighing from about fifteen to fifty pounds apiece. They were big, but it wasn't nearly as many fish as I'd caught the time before.

The fishing business became somewhat lucrative—we were at least making enough money to pay the mortgage and utilities and take care of the rest of our needs—but I still didn't believe it was my, ahem, calling in life. I kept going back to a memorable hunting trip I'd made with Al Bolen a few years earlier outside of Junction City, Arkansas. A large flock of mallard ducks had flown high above us, and I hit them with a long, hailing call when they were on their way out of sight. I turned the flock, and it began to circle, dipping lower as the ducks approached our decoys and blind. When the ducks began to sail wide, I hit them again with a short *chop-chop* that turned them back toward our blind, where we waited. The flock dropped into the water directly in front of us, in perfect gun range.

When the shooting was over, Big Al told me, "Man, you weren't calling those ducks, you were *commanding* them!"

Al, who knew of my tinkering with his and other hunters' duck calls, urged me to make my own and sell them.

"And I've got the name for it: Duck Commander," Big Al told me.

> Big Al told me, "Man, you weren't calling those ducks, you were commanding them!"

I was struck by the phrase and it never left my mind: Duck Commander. It sort of has a ring to it, doesn't it?

Duck Commander was always in the back of my mind, its implementation only awaiting a trigger. When Kay and I were discussing our future one night, I told her that I wanted to build and sell duck calls but would continue to fish until I got the duck-call business off the ground.

"I don't know how I'm going to build the duck-call sales yet, but I'll figure that out. When they get to where we don't need to fish anymore, we'll be on our way," I told her.

## Sportsman's Paradise

The move to Sportsman's Paradise and my commercial fishing had turned out well. Our family was together again, and I was thriving both spiritually and emotionally. Would another life-changing gamble work again? With the good Lord behind the steering wheel, we were about to find out.

# DUCK COMMANDER

*Rule No. 8 for Living Happy, Happy, Happy*
Never Sell Yourself Short
(You Never Know, You Might Become a Millionaire)

**S**ome of the most successful businesses in American history started as mom-and-pop operations, on nothing more than a family's dream, hard work, and a shoestring budget. Ben & Jerry's Ice Cream opened its first store in a run-down gas station in Burlington, Vermont, in 1978. It was sold for $326 million to a competitor in 2000. Walmart started as a five-and-dime store in Bentonville, Arkansas, in 1950 before Sam Walton and his family created the world's biggest retailer. In 1946, S. Truett Cathy opened a single restaurant, a twenty-four-hour diner outside of Atlanta, which was so small it had only ten stools and four tables. He and his brother named it the Dwarf Grill. Today, Chick-fil-A sells more than $4 billion in chicken sandwiches and other food annually across the country.

Like those businesses, Duck Commander was nothing more

than a dream when I decided to launch the company. Obviously, I had no idea the business would become what it is today, but I had the courage and determination to believe we could compete with the more established companies in the duck-call industry, some of which had been manufacturing calls since the early twentieth century. My idea of starting Duck Commander began when Al Bolen made his comments about my ability to command ducks on the water. But it was during another hunting trip that my business finally started to come to fruition.

Baxter Brasher, a fellow member of White's Ferry Road Church and an executive of Howard Brothers Discount Stores, where Kay worked, asked me to take him duck-hunting. Brasher had noticed a lot of men and boys asking me questions about hunting, fishing, and duck calls before and after church, and he was curious to find out what all the fuss was about. After I showed him how it was done, Brasher was even more impressed. He told me, "You really, really ought to build a duck call."

I told him I had a design and a plan to do it but didn't have the money to make it happen.

"Well, how much money would you need?" Brasher asked.

So I asked around and checked on the price of equipment and everything else I would need. I went back to Brasher and told him it would cost about $25,000 for me to get into the duck-call business.

"Twenty-five thousand?" Brasher asked me as he shuffled some papers on his desk. "Let me see. Here's what you do: You take this piece of paper—it's my financial statement—and you take it down to the bank. Walk in there and tell them you want twenty-five thousand dollars. They're going to say, 'Do you have any collateral?' You hand them this piece of paper and say, 'There is my collateral right there. He's backing me.'"

I asked Brasher, "How much do you want?"

> I told him I had a design and a plan to do it but didn't have the money to make it happen.

"I don't want anything," he told me. "The reason I don't want anything is I know it'll work. You'll do well. I don't want a dime. I want to know I helped someone get started. You just go down there and tell them what you need."

So I went down to the bank and walked in, and a clerk asked if she could help me.

"I need to see Mr. George Campbell, the man who loans the money," I told her.

She walked me back to Campbell's office and he asked, "How can I help you?"

"I need twenty-five thousand dollars," I told him. "I'm going into the duck-call business."

"Mr. Robertson, what do you have for collateral?" he asked me.

I laid that piece of paper down on Campbell's desk just like Brasher told me to do and answered, "There's my collateral."

I never will forget what happened next. Campbell looked at the paper and looked at the name. Then he said, "Brenda, will you get us some coffee?"

*Now we're getting somewhere,* I thought to myself. He went from "who are you," "what do you want," and "where's your collateral" to "let's have coffee."

Duck Commander—and my dream of building my own duck calls—was about to take flight.

After I had the bank loan, I went into high gear looking for the machinery I would need. By chance, I ran across a classified in the back of a magazine that was advertising a lathe, which is a woodworking machine I needed to build the barrels for my duck calls. I called the seller to inquire about the lathe he was trying to get rid of.

"How much money do you have to spend on this, Mr. Robertson?" the guy asked me.

"Well, I only have about twenty-five thousand," I told him.

"You're in luck, Mr. Robertson," the man replied. "The equipment is only $24,985."

The sucker fleeced me! The lathe was worth maybe five thousand dollars, but he took everything I had for it. It's one of the reasons we were so poor during the first ten years of operating

Duck Commander. Everything we made was going back to the bank to pay for the lathe! I later learned the lathe was built in the 1920s. It was originally used in Chicago and was in Memphis, Tennessee, when I bought it. The equipment was out-of-date. It was an old-fashioned, flat-knife lathe, but thankfully it actually worked pretty well once I got it hooked up and running.

While I waited for the lathe to arrive, I finalized my model for a duck call. I was able to call ducks from the time I was very young. I learned as a teenager using a P. S. Olt D-2 duck call, which was designed by Philip Stanford Olt of Pekin, Illinois, in the early 1900s. It was an Arkansas-style call, which is a one-piece insert with a straight reed and curved tone board. I always had a knack for making a call sound right or better. My hunting buddies were always asking me to tune, adjust, or repair their calls, and they always seemed to sound more like a duck when I finished tinkering with them.

When I decided to make my own duck calls, I enlisted the help of Tommy Powell, who went to our church. Tommy's father, John Spurgeon Powell, made duck calls, and I went to him with my concept of how one should be built. John Spurgeon Powell looked at my specifications and concluded that my call wouldn't work; he told me it was too small. But he promised me if I could get the hole drilled properly, he would turn it on his lathe and make me a call.

A lot of new ideas were going into what I was asking him to build: mine would be a smaller caller and would have a double reed, which I thought were significant improvements. The call's barrel size, thickness, and a few other specifications were to come later as I refined it. One other big improvement was actually Pa's idea, and I'm not sure I would have ever come up with it. The double reeds had a tendency to stick together, so Pa suggested we put a dimple in the bottom reed to eliminate the problem.

So we took a nail, rounded off the point, and with a hammer tapped a little dimple in the reed. When assembled with the protruded dimple of the bottom reed against the top reed, it worked perfectly. We later made a small tool from a sewing kit and just pressed the dimple into the reeds we were making. To this day, with all the automation that has come into the making of Duck Commander calls, Si, who has worked for the company since retiring from the army, still puts the dimples in the reeds by hand, one at a time.

Si, who has worked for the company since retiring from the army, still puts the dimples in the reeds by hand, one at a time.

After my meeting with John Spurgeon Powell, I cut a little six-inch-long, three-inch-square block of wood but still needed someone to drill a hole in it. To get it done, I took the block to nearby West Monroe High School's woodworking shop. The shop teacher told me he didn't have time to fool with it.

I told him, "Four dressed mallard ducks for that hole."

"Good night! Now we're talking!" he replied.

I gave him four dressed mallard ducks to drill a hole that took him just a matter of seconds. That was the beginning of my first duck call. John Spurgeon Powell turned it on his lathe and finished it off for me. I had a prototype to build what I guessed would be millions more one day.

After a few weeks, a train brought the lathe to West Monroe, and I drove my pickup to the depot yard and backed it up to the loading dock. As I got out of the truck, I told a man on the dock to load up my shipment.

"You the one here after that equipment—that machine for the duck deal?" he asked me.

"Yeah," I told him.

"Son, have you seen it?" he asked.

"Nah. I don't have any idea what it looks like," I said.

"Well, have you ever run any machinery like that?" he asked again.

"Nah, I'm going to figure that out when I see it," I said.

"Well, first of all, you ain't going to haul it in no pickup truck," he informed me. "Son, you need a flatbed—a big truck."

"Really?" I asked.

I walked back into the warehouse and looked at it. Good night! It was *iron*! I thought it was going to be little stuff, you know—for duck calls. But the machinery was huge—and heavy. It looked to me like it covered an acre back there. I never found out what it was built to turn, but it must have been something big!

I immediately borrowed a ragged dump truck I saw among several at the depot. It belonged to one of the members at church who happened to work there. I backed the truck up to the dock. I remember the depot crew standing there looking at me like I was deranged, but they loaded the lathe onto the truck for me. Away went the Duck Commander.

But further problems lay ahead of me at home. I had planned to put the lathe in a small building on my property that I was using for a shop. It measured about twelve feet by twelve feet. When I arrived with the men I'd gotten to drive the truck home and help unload, one man looked at the building dubiously and said, "It's not going in there—not through that door."

I said, "Oh yeah, it'll go in there." I got out my chain saw and stuck the snout of it into the north wall and went to cutting. *Whannnnnnnn!* I was cutting through nails and everything. They were all just standing back, looking at me like they were witnessing the Texas Chain Saw Massacre. I kept at it. *Whannnnnnnn!*

When I finished cutting my way to the top of both sides, *ka-whooom!* The whole wall fell out!

I backed the truck up to the shed, dropped the dump gate, and hooked one end of a come-along to the lathe and the other end to a tree. I dragged the heavy iron machine inside the shop. It filled the available space from end to end, leaving just enough room in front of it for an operator. We set the wall back in place and nailed it up. All in all, it was a successful operation. It's amazing what a little redneck engineering can do!

I anchored the lathe down, leaving it on the original shipping skids. It operated that way as long as it was in use. The equipment was so heavy that, within a couple of years, its weight caused the shop to sink a foot into the ground. But the lathe remained relatively level as it sank, so its operation wasn't affected. Nothing was ever done about releveling the shop.

By now it was dark outside. It had been a long day. Despite all the setbacks, I had overcome my obstacles and was exultant. The factory to make the duck calls wasn't operating yet, but everything was in place.

I was so excited about our future that I went down the hill to see Pa and Granny. They were seated at the table, playing dominoes with Alan and Jase—they played dominoes together nearly every night. Pa believed in playing dominoes with children because it taught them to add rapidly and develop strategy, thinking several moves ahead. Whether the dominoes did that or not, all the boys did well in mathematics and the rest of their school subjects.

Now, I told y'all I talk pretty dramatically when the situation warrants it, and this was maybe the biggest day of my life. I walked into my parents' house and announced to everyone, "Y'all see this duck call right here?"

I was holding the call John Spurgeon Powell built for me. Of course, they all stopped and were looking at me.

"I'm in the process of getting these duplicated on that equipment out there," I told them. "Read my lips: we're going to sell a million dollars' worth of these things before it's over."

Pa was sitting there—and they're all still looking at me. When I said we were going to sell a million dollars' worth, they all looked back down at their dominoes. Pa picked one up, smacked it on the table, and said, "Ten!" He didn't even acknowledge what I'd said!

None of them said "Good night," "That sounds great," or anything! They just kept playing. I walked out, thinking to myself, *Well, I didn't get any of them fired up.* And I thought, *Well, maybe not a million dollars' worth.*

Sometimes I still think about telling Pa I was going to make a million dollars—and that his only response was to take a ten-count. Since that time, as it turned out, we have sold way more than that. Who would have believed me at the time?

Undaunted, I set to work the next day trying to get the lathe running. It was a harder task than I envisioned. Coupled with my and Pa's lack of knowledge about running a lathe (Pa did show interest in the project once it got under way) was the fact that it came with no instruction manual on how to operate it.

I had never run a lathe, but I saw a button that said Start. It's like Jase says: when you don't know what you're doing, it's best to do it quickly! So I pressed the button, and that thing fired up. Good grief! There were big old belts spinning with no protection on them, and the whole thing was humming! I saw a big handle, and I wondered what would happen if I pulled it up. *Whiiizzzzzz!* All these blades and metal parts started moving. I said, "Whoa, whoa, now!" and shut her down. Remember what I said about on and off buttons? Fortunately, the lathe was old enough to still have them!

> It's like Jase says: when you don't know what you're doing, it's best to do it quickly!

I had never seen such a thing before. I didn't have a book. Nobody was there. I didn't know how to set anything. So I just went a little bit at a time. The first thing I did was call some cat from the company that built it. When I started telling him what I was trying to do, he said, "Aw, naw, naw, man! You've got to have templates."

"What?" I asked him.

"You've got to have some templates," he repeated.

And then he started explaining what they were and how that thing worked. After that, it was trial and error to get everything working right. I hadn't been sent any templates, or jigs as some call them, which are thin metal plates used as guides to cut wood accurately into the shape you want. So I acquired what we needed.

Let me tell you: we tore up some wood out there. You wouldn't believe the pile of shavings and waste. But Pa and I were determined to make it work.

While we were getting the lathe lined up and figuring out how it worked, I came up with another idea. I decided that maybe I could get someone to build my duck calls for me so I could start selling them. At least there would still be some money coming in, while we figured out how to build our own.

I was already testing the market and had traveled to quite a few areas, including my old hometown of Vivian, as well as places in eastern Texas, southern Arkansas, western Mississippi, and as far away as the bayou parts of southern Louisiana. It was in Lake Charles, Louisiana, that I encountered Alan J. Earhart, who had been making the Cajun Game Call. It was an old duck call, and he had been building it for years. Earhart was sympathetic to my quest, so we made a deal from which both of us benefited.

Earhart agreed to build two thousand Duck Commanders at a price of two dollars each, while I was getting my equipment lined up. Earhart had his own lathe, and he switched it over to build my calls. Earhart said that of all the people he had met starting out in the duck-call business, he thought I had enough energy and drive to pull it off.

"But man," he told me. "You've got a long way to go."

I had no idea exactly how long it would take me to get Duck Commander to where it is today.

# FAMILY BUSINESS

*Rule No. 9 for Living Happy, Happy, Happy*
It's Cheaper to Hire Your Relatives
(Unless You Don't Like 'Em)

**P**eople ask me all the time about the early days of Duck Commander, when it was just Pa, Kay, the boys, and me trying to learn how to operate a heavy lathe and build duck calls in a small woodshop outside our home. I'm sure that at various times Kay and everyone else assumed I was crazy, and they were probably right.

Like my childhood, our company started from humble, humble beginnings. When we first started fishing the Ouachita River, it was so slow you might see two buzzards fighting over an inner tube! When we ran out of roadkill to bait our nets, the buzzards fought over anything else they could find! After we launched Duck Commander, our first year of sales totaled only eight thousand dollars. I told Kay, "I know I have a master's degree, but I'm gonna stay the course on this one. I think this will work. If the Almighty is with us, it will work." It was just like when I persuaded her to move out next to the river, so I could give up my teaching job to become a commercial fisherman. I told her then, "If you get me a place on the river, I'll fish the river. I'll be the smartest commercial fisherman out there."

Of course, everybody laughed at us in the early days. People would come by our house and say, "Let me get this right: you have a master's degree from Louisiana Tech University, you could've played professional football, but you turned that down so you could do *what*?"

I always told them that I was fishing the river and following my dream. I got seventy cents a pound on the catfish and thirty cents a pound on the buffalo, which wasn't a bad living. I was determined to see it through until the duck call business was big enough to support us, and then I would hang my fishing nets up for good. A lot of my friends tell me they thought I was a complete idiot.

Now I ask them, "Well, it's forty years since you thought I was an idiot; what about now?" Now they're calling me a genius! Boy, it took forty years for them to turn, but now they finally say, "That old guy ain't as dumb as he looks."

I remember making a speech somewhere and a man walking up to me after I was finished. He said, "Mr. Robertson, I'll tell you what I got out of that speech: You're kind of like one of them old Airedale terrier dogs. You ain't as dumb as you look!"

I told the guy, "Man, I appreciate those words of wisdom." I laughed at that one; that was a good one.

I might not be the most intelligent guy on Earth, but I always had the where-withal, determination, and work ethic to turn my business into a success, or at least to make it profitable enough to feed and care for my family, which is really all I ever wanted.

"Well, it's forty years since you thought I was an idiot; what about now?" Now they're calling me a genius!

When the serious work started at Duck Commander, I installed a shed roof on the south side of our workshop to shelter a heavy-duty table saw my brother Tommy loaned me to help get the business going. Shavings and sawdust always covered the floor in untidy piles. In one area were cedar shavings, which were cut while we made the end-piece blanks of the duck calls. In another pile was the walnut residue sheared off the call barrels, which I turned on the lathe inside my shop. Several cedar and walnut logs, the woods from which the original Duck Commander calls were made, were piled up in front.

But the most noticeable addition, and the first thing visitors saw when they came to our house, was the roughly lettered sign that proclaimed DUCK COMMANDER WORLDWIDE. I took an old board, painted it white, and lettered it with black. Then I nailed it up at an angle, which I did for a little bit of show (remember what I said about being dramatic?). People would come out to our house, see the sign above the shop door, and walk around wondering, "What have you got out there?" More than four decades later the sign still hangs in front of our property.

Obviously, there was a lot of learning on the job, including enough errors and corrections to drive me nearly mad. But it didn't take us long to get a production line going, and Alan, Jase, Willie, Kay, and Pa were my crew. Our assembly line was out on the porch of our house, which was screened in at the time. Pa was always helping me. Willie was the youngest, so his job was to sweep up the sawdust in the shop. My oldest son, Alan, was given a little more responsibility—he used a band saw to cut the ends of the calls. Then I ran a drill press to set up and calibrate the end pieces.

Jase and Willie also dipped the calls in polyurethane and dried them on nails, which wasn't a very fun job. They hung the calls on a piece of plywood, eight feet by four feet, which leaned against one of the big pine trees in our yard. Neat rows of four-inch finishing nails were driven into the plywood, about two inches apart, from top to bottom. They'd open a five-gallon bucket of polyurethane, insert their fingers into the ends of duck-call barrels until they had four on each hand, then dip them into the thick liquid—submerging a little of their fingers to make sure the resin coated the barrels completely. With a light touch so as not to mar the finish, they worked each one off their fingers as they placed them carefully and separately on protruding nails. Then they repeated the operation until the entire board was filled with shiny, coated duck-call barrels drying in the open air.

It was a very tedious job, and a big one for boys who were so young, but it was all part of our quest to build the best duck calls in the industry. The dipping ensured a smooth, clear, permanent coat of resin that protected the wood. Sometimes, there would be one little rough spot at the mouthpiece end where the barrel touched a nail. When that happened, it had to be sanded smooth before the call could be sold. Once the calls were dry, the boys sanded them down to a fine finish. I think my boys were a little embarrassed going to school with their fingers stained brown from tung oil, but it was one of the hazards of the job. There were always rows of hard tung-oil drippings in our yard, and the trunks of the trees were covered in tung oil. The especially bad part for them was when I figured out that the more you sanded and dipped the calls, the shinier they were. That meant even more dipping!

Last, and most important, I blew every single call to make sure it sounded like a duck. From day one, I was convinced my duck call sounded more like a live duck than anything else on the market, and I wanted to make sure my products were always perfect. A small flaw in appearance wasn't critical, but not so in sound. It had to sound like a mallard hen, which was the standard I established for my calls. Duck Commander still follows that same principle today. A faulty call was either fixed or rejected. We used the rejects as fire starters in our wood heater for years.

Another early problem we had to overcome was packaging. We didn't have any! In fact, I didn't even have my name on the calls. I went up to the paper mill in West Monroe, and they built me sheets of flat boxes we could cut out and then fold it into shape, in which a duck call would fit neatly. The boxes were plain white with no writing on them.

Armed with my first boxed duck calls, I left home to flood the market. The first sale of Duck Commander calls was to Gene Lutz of Gene's Sporting Goods in Monroe, and the next was to Harold Katz in Alexandria, Louisiana. Then I drove over to Lorant's Sporting Goods in Shreveport, Louisiana, a reputable old hunting store that had been in business for years. I walked in and was able to see Mr. Lorant, the owner. I put my boxed duck calls on the counter and asked him, "How many of these duck calls do you want?"

Lorant picked up a couple and looked them over. Then he

looked up at me dubiously and asked, "You want me to buy these?"

"Yeah, put them on the market," I told him. "They're Duck Commanders, and I'm going into the business."

He looked at them again and said, "Where's the name on them? You don't have any printing on your box?"

"Nah, they'll find out who I am," I replied.

Lorant paused a minute, then said to me in all seriousness, "Son, let me give you some advice: get some printing on your boxes. You have to have some printing on your box. You are not going to do any good with that."

Then Lorant told me he'd buy six of them. It was the beginning of a good relationship. Once we started building them, Lorant went on to sell thousands—tens of thousands of dollars' worth.

> "Son, let me give you some advice: get some printing on your boxes."

I took Lorant's advice to heart, and our packaging became a priority. We had an attractive box printed, which was covered with a transparent plastic top that showcased the duck call. Visible through the top of the box when it was placed properly on a shelf was the duck call and its now-famous logo: a mallard drake with wings cupped and legs lowered, looking down to the land. There was even an attractive sticker affixed to the barrel of the duck call. The first logo drawings were printed in gold on a green background. "Duck Commander," "Phil Robertson," and my Luna, Louisiana, address were easily visible.

Over the next few years, many evenings were spent inside our house, with me blowing Duck Commanders and the rest of the family cutting boxes, folding them, and filling them with the approved calls. No one was exempt from folding boxes. If you came to our house, you were probably going to participate in packaging—after eating one of Kay's delicious home-cooked meals, of course. It was a sociable time, and everyone talked and enjoyed it as they worked, while tuning out my duck-call blowing. Eventually, I also pressed my brothers into service, and each took his turn on the lathe at one time or another, using the templates to turn out barrels and end pieces.

Even in the early days of the operation, I was planning for our future. As the early Duck Commanders were being built, I carefully measured the calls that sounded just like I wanted with micrometers and calipers, recording and saving the dimensions for the time when we would build molded plastic calls. My database was eventually used to design a uniform product that eliminated the flaws inherent in wood.

But even today, many waterfowl hunters still prefer the wooden calls, and sometimes their sound is superior. At one point, we were doing well enough that I wanted to recall the first calls we made because they were so crude looking. They weren't nearly as well done as the newer ones—either wood or plastic. I just wanted to get them out of sight. Some of them looked pretty ragged, and I figured they would hurt future sales. Using a list Kay kept of our customers, we sent out a letter offering them a new Duck Commander if they would send their old one back to us.

I was amazed. The offer was met with suspicion as to what we were up to. Hunters from all over were calling or writing to say they wouldn't part with their calls for anything. They told us they were the "originals," and they weren't going to give them up. We were surprised how quickly we'd established brand loyalty among our customers.

The early marketing of Duck Commander depended strictly on me, although I enlisted my brother Tommy to call on some stores in the East Texas area where he lived. I traveled in a four-state area, driving through Arkansas, Louisiana, Mississippi, and Texas. I stopped in each town I passed through, calling on small sporting goods stores, hardware stores, five-and-dime stores—any business that looked like it might have an interest in selling duck calls. I did it from an old blue and white Ford Fairlane 500 that Kay inherited from Nannie. While Alan was driving it one time, a delivery truck sideswiped it, and the whole left side—fender, door, and back panel—was gone. Neither vehicle stopped, and I chose to ignore the accident. But the Ford still ran well and was carrying the first Duck Commanders to market.

I had one big selling tool—besides my loveable personality and redneck charm, that is. I made a recording of live mallard ducks calling and then added the sound of me blowing on a Duck Commander as a comparison. I tried to sell the idea that I was closer to sounding like a duck than anyone in the world.

My approach was successful. After we sold $8,000 worth of Duck Commanders the first year, we sold $13,500 the second year. The next year, we sold $22,000. I told Kay, "We are now rolling." The next year we sold about $35,000. We didn't hit six figures until about ten years after we started, but the business grew bigger every year.

Out of that first year's sales, I made about a dollar on each duck call. We were selling them to the stores for $4.27 wholesale. I figured they cost me about $3.20 total, after paying Mr. Earhart to build them, travel, paperwork, and all. We did a lot better when we began to build them ourselves.

About the third year after I started, I decided I was going about the selling all wrong. I felt I needed to go to Stuttgart, Arkansas, the duck capital of the world. I had been driving around trying to interest these little old sporting goods stores. I needed to raise my sights and become a little more ambitious. So I took my tape and cassette player, climbed in the old Ford, and headed for Stuttgart, 185 miles away. I pulled up in front of the only sporting goods store in town, a little bitty place.

I got out with my tape recorder, the live ducks comparison, and some duck calls strung around my neck.

*I needed to raise my sights and become a little more ambitious.*

I walked into the store and there were two guys sitting at a table. I was about to learn they were world-champion duck callers, who just happened to be sitting in the store. The fellow behind the counter asked me if he could help me.

"Is this the duck capital of the world?" I asked him.

"You're here," he said with a proud smile on his face.

"Well, I figure this is where I need to start," I told him. "Now, here's the deal. I have a duck call here—hanging around my neck. It's closer to a duck than any duck call that has ever been made. Do y'all want to hear it?"

They all looked at each other and kind of grinned.

"Let me guess," the guy behind the counter said. "You're out of Louisiana?"

"That's where I'm from," I said.

"Blow that thing," the guy told me.

I blew one of the calls around my neck, concentrating on the plain, simple sound of the mallard hen with no frills. I understood I was blowing for an audience conditioned by duck-calling contests, which often featured forty-note high calls that not only taxed a caller's lung power but also made the rafters ring. The "lonesome hen" call blown by contestants would make you weep. They could make a duck call talk. But I was making the outlandish claim that they didn't sound like a duck.

They listened. Then they chuckled, kind of laughed. They were still chuckling when the guy behind the counter picked up my duck call, blew on it, and said, "I see your problem with this duck call right off the bat."

"What's the problem?" I asked him.

"Air leaks a little bit around here," he told me. "You've got an air leak."

"That's the way it's designed," I responded. "Air leaks and all, it's still closer to a duck than anybody's."

I turned to the men at the table and asked if they duck-hunted.

"Yeah, we do a little duck-hunting," one of them told me.

"These guys are world-champion duck callers," explained the man behind the counter, with the proper amount of respect in his voice.

"Well, good night!" I exclaimed. "Boys, let's have us a contest right here. Get your duck calls and get up here. We'll tape your duck calls beside that of these live ducks. I've already got mine on it. We'll listen to the ducks, then all the calls. Then we'll just vote on it. Whoever is closest to a duck wins!"

The guy behind the counter looked and me and said, "You see that door there? Hit it!"

He ran me out of there! But as I was driving out of town, frustrated and still fuming over my reception in a little nondescript sporting goods store, I saw a beer joint with about fifteen cars parked around it. On an impulse, I wheeled my car into the parking lot, squealing to a stop.

I walked in the door and hollered, "Hey!"

The customers were all sitting around drinking beer. They turned and looked at me.

"Is there a duck caller in the house?" I asked loudly.

They all looked at me like they were deaf.

"Is there anybody in here who can blow a duck call?" I asked again.

Several of the customers pointed to a man sitting and quietly having a beer. He looked around at me.

"Come out here, I want to show you a duck call that I built," I told him. "I want you to tell me how I can sell these things up here. They just ran me out of the sporting goods store down there."

"They did?" the man asked with bewilderment in his voice. "Yeah, let me listen to it."

He went outside with me. I blew my call for him.

"Son, let me tell you something," the man told me. "I've been blowing duck calls for a long time. My hunting call is a Yentzen—until now. How much you want for one of them things?"

"Ten dollars," I told him.

"I want one right now," he said.

"No, I'm going to give it to you," I told him.

The man invited me to his house. I introduced myself to him and followed him back through town.

"Robertson, let me tell you something," he told me later. "These guys up here are making big money selling these world-championship duck calls. They don't want any ten-dollar duck calls up here in their way. To them, they're so far above you. What they are going to tell you is that unless you win the world championship blowing like they did, you're never going to sell any duck calls."

"But their calls don't sound like ducks," I told him.

"I know they don't," he replied. "But they have a deal going here, a clique, and they're making big money."

"So what do you think I should do?" I asked him.

"Aw, you'll sell duck calls," he replied. "You'll end up selling way more than they will. I've heard a lot of duck calls. But I've never heard one that sounded closer to a duck than that. That thing is a duck! These guides up here, the ones that hunt, they'll buy them. So will all serious duck hunters. You're just going to have to stay the course."

You know what? I don't remember the man's name; I only recall that he was a rice farmer. But his advice and encouragement carried me a long way over the next few years. About ten years later, when I developed a mallard drake call, a few of them were ordered by that little sporting goods store in Stuttgart. I guess they finally realized my call sounded like a duck.

The guy behind the counter in that store wasn't the only one who had doubts about the Duck Commanders. It probably took me twenty-five years to convince the duck-calling world that there is a difference between meat calling and contest calling.

The Duck Commander has come a long way. But it hasn't been easy.

Somehow, we stayed the course and it turned out. There is a God, and He blessed us because we did what was right—we loved Him, we loved our neighbor, and we hunted ducks. He is real and what He said He would do is what happened. He said, you love Me and do what's right, and I'll bless you—so much so that your barns will be full, packed full, tapped down, and running over. I only know that either our success came from Him or

> It probably took me twenty-five years to convince the duck-calling world that there is a difference between meat calling and contest calling.

I was one of the luckiest souls that ever came along with a little idea. All I can say is it's one or the other, but I'm leaning toward the Almighty doing exactly what He said He would do.

The Almighty blessed us, and Duck Commander did work, just like He said it would. Yes, it took a long, long time for us to get to where we are today. But even before our success, and long before *Duck Dynasty* came along, everybody was happy, happy, happy. In other words, it wasn't like my love for the Almighty was contingent upon whether the blessings came or not. My prayer was always: "Lord, if You bless me, I'll thank You; but if You don't, I'll be thankful for what I have. I have plenty. I'm in good shape." Even before our success came along, we had air-conditioning, color TV, hot water, and a bathtub. We had everything we needed. When I was a boy, we didn't even have bathtubs or commodes, but I was still as happy and content as I am today. As long as I was doing what God said was right and living my life for Him, I knew everything would work out in the end—one way or another.

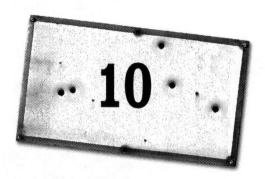

# IF IT SOUNDS
# LIKE A DUCK . . .

*Rule No. 10 for Living Happy, Happy, Happy*
If You're Going to Do Something, Do It Right
(Instead of Doing It Again)

**W**hen I was a bit of a wild child during the 1960s, one of my favorite musicians was Jimi Hendrix. A masterful showman, Hendrix was a brilliant experimentalist and one of the most influential musicians in history. Hendrix had an incredible ability to manipulate a six-string guitar and distort it to make sounds no one would have believed possible. You know what was most amazing about Hendrix? That sucker never learned to read music! He learned to play guitar by ear but did more with it than anyone before him or anyone since.

Now imagine trying to replicate a duck's sound by ear—without a duck's bill! When we're building duck calls, we try to use the same methods as people trying to learn to play music by ear. They can't read musical notes or charts, but when they hear notes, they memorize them, and then they sit down at a piano and play exactly what they heard. They duplicate the sounds in their heads and play them from memory. We do the same thing with duck calls. We hear 'em while we're out hunting, and then we build a device that sounds exactly like what we heard. Just like on a piano, we have to make sure we have the right pitch, note, inflection, and volume to ensure that our duck calls sound exactly like a mallard, green-winged teal, wood duck, American wigeon, or whatever duck species we're trying to imitate.

It isn't easy, and it requires a lot of trial and error to get a duck call to sound exactly right. After all, it's not like we were trying to replicate Daffy Duck—*thufferin' thuccotash!* Each duck species has a very unique and distinct sound; you can't call a wood duck with a green-winged teal call or vice versa. And this probably won't surprise you, but female ducks always sound different from males, even if they're of the same species.

Despite all the variations in sounds, what we've discovered over the years is that if a duck whistles, then you use a whistle to duplicate the sound. If a duck quacks, you use a call with a reed in it. One species of duck—the gadwall—requires both a whistle and a reed.

We build calls for all kinds of ducks. There is a certain percentage of waterfowl hunters who are mallard purists, but we appreciate all ducks. Of course, there are a few species that we'll draw the line on and won't eat. We don't eat the common merganser, and I understand there are particular sea ducks that are nearly inedible. For us, it's just as much fun to hunt wood ducks as mallards or green-winged teals. I think the most elegant, graceful duck is the pintail. For good table fare, our favorite ducks are the green-winged teals and close behind them are the wood ducks. If we really want a good duck gumbo or duck with dressing, we almost always go for the green-winged teal. They go fast around our table, especially if Willie has pulled up a chair!

> The green-winged teals go fast around our table, especially if Willie has pulled up a chair!

Of course, the species I dislike the most is the Steven Seagal ducks—the ones that are hard to kill!

The very first duck call I made in 1972 was the Original Commander Call, which was designed for the mallard hen. The mallard is probably the most recognizable of all ducks and is the ancestor of many of the breeds we see in the United States. The mallard hen is covered in feathers of uneven hues from buff to very dark brown and usually has a brown or orange bill. The male mallard has a white neck ring, which separates its distinctive green head from its chestnut-brown chest. The rest of its body is mottled in lighter brown to gray to black, and its speculum feathers are a distinct purple-blue with black and white edging. The male mallard's bill is yellow, and its legs and feet are bright coral red. The male mallard is really a beautiful bird. Of course, that doesn't stop me from dropping them from the sky whenever I'm given the chance!

I made the mallard-hen call first because most ducks will respond to that kind of sound. We still make the Original Commander Call today, and each one tends to sounds different because every one is still made by hand from wood. Of course we still blow on every call to make sure it sounds exactly right. The Original Commander Call is the quintessential duck "quack," and the mallard hen typically gives the call in a series of two to ten quacks that start loud and get softer as she goes (sounds a lot like a woman I know at home). Now, not all mallard hens sound exactly the same. When you're blowing on an Original Commander Call to attract a mallard hen, you can quicken and sharpen the cadence to replicate a young mallard hen, or slow down and draw out the cadence to get an old, raspy mallard hen. There are three distinctive sounds for a mallard hen: quack, feed call, and hail call. The mallard hen call is very versatile and effective.

The Mallard Drake Call came along next. We were the first company to build one, so we patented it so our competitors couldn't copy our design. The male mallard doesn't quack; it's more of a quiet, raspy sound. When I set out to build the Mallard Drake, I superglued various sizes of PVC pipe together and finally mastered it. When I finally built a call that sounded exactly like a male mallard, I went tearing into our house and told Miss Kay, "I have it! We're going to revolutionize duck calls as we know them!"

I blew on the Mallard Drake Call for her.

"What is that?" she asked me. "Is it a frog?"

If you blow too high on a Mallard Drake Call, you really do sound like a tree frog—and there's no meat on those suckers! You have to catch the plump bullfrogs if you want a meal. The Mallard Drake Call is different from any other duck call. With most calls, you say, "Ten, ten, ten," while you're blowing into it. But with the Mallard Drake, you're basically saying, "Aaaaah," on a very low bass note as you raise your fingers off the call. It's an easy thing to do, unless you're a tenor. The Mallard Drake Call is controlled by your vocal cords and is really a whistle with a stem on it. You have to remember that when you're on an amplifier, whether it's with a guitar or any other musical instrument, you get maximum vibration when you hit a bass note. So you have to go really, really low when you're calling mallard drakes.

Conversely, there are three types of ducks that are whistlers: teal, wigeon, and pintail. Believe it or not, I built our first whistle from a children's musical toy set. None of the flutes and horns in the toy set sounded like a duck, but after I spent an hour with a band saw and used plenty of superglue, I built a whistle that sounded like six birds! For pintails, you put your finger in the opening while you're blowing; for wigeons and teals, you blow straight into the whistle. You can even use our whistle to call mallard drakes, doves, or quails if you want. That's why we call our whistle a six-in-one call.

The green-winged teal is the smallest of the North American dabbling ducks. It has a short neck and small bill, and its chestnut head has a green eye patch that extends to the nape of its neck. It's another pretty bird. Male green-winged teals have a high-pitched, single-note *peep* sound, while females are relatively quiet. But the females will let out a sharp, high-pitched quack when they're flushed. Like most women, you'll know when they've been bothered! When you're calling a green-winged teal, you don't do it very loud, and you use fine, little short notes while you're blowing air directly into the whistle. It's almost like a miniature mallard hen call, but when you get four or five people *peep*ing at the same time, it's exactly what teals sound like on the water.

There are also blue-winged teals and cinnamon teals, and they're identifiable by the colors their names suggest. The blue-winged teals, which have blue-gray upper wings, are common in the northern prairies and parklands of the central United States. We see a few blue-winged teals every once in a while, but they tend to winter farther to the south. The male has a high-whistled *tsee, tsee* sound, while the female lets out loud, evenly spaced quacks. The blue-winged teals are a lot of fun to hunt because they fly very fast and make erratic twists and turns as they fly low over your decoy spreads. The cinnamon teal, which has a cinnamon-red head, neck, breast, and belly, are common around the Great Salt Lake in Utah and the central valleys of California. They winter in Mexico and other parts of Central America, so we don't see them in Louisiana. The male cinnamon teal makes a series of *chuk* notes, while the female gives off more of a quack.

We see a lot of American wigeons, which are also known as baldpates and have a bluish gray-tipped bill. The males have a white crown on their heads and a green face patch. The wigeon drake gives out three high, squeaky whistles, like *whee, whee, whee.* To call a male wigeon, you stick the whistle in the corner of your mouth and clench your teeth. You blow three times and make sure you accent the second sound. The female wigeon, which has a gray head with a brownish-black crown, gives out a quack sound. We usually end up seeing a lot of American wigeon ducks; they nest in parts of Canada and are usually the first to migrate south for the winter.

The northern pintail is a long, slim duck with long, narrow wings, a slender neck, and a long tail. You can't mistake a pintail for any other kind of duck. Some people call them the "greyhounds of the air," and the males have chocolate-brown heads with a white stripe on each side of their necks. The male lets out growling, guttural notes, and they're not easy to duplicate. If you look in the mirror, you'll see a round piece of meat hanging in the back of your throat. God gave us that piece of meat to call a pintail duck. If we didn't have it and couldn't flutter it as we blew air into a whistle, we'd sound like a backhoe backing up: *beep, beep, beep!* But because God gave us that piece of meat, we can sound exactly like a pintail duck. The female pintail quacks and sounds nothing like a male.

Now, I can't take credit for all the duck calls that Duck Commander has developed over the years. One time when my son Jase was hunting with me, he had a mallard hen call in one corner of his mouth and a whistle in the other and was blowing them at the same time. As Jase was blowing on both of them, a flight of gadwalls turned and came right down to our decoys. After we shot 'em, I asked Jase, "What were you doing down there? It sounded like a gadwall."

> Jase had a mallard hen call in one corner of his mouth and a whistle in the other and was blowing them at the same time.

"Why do you think they came down here?" Jase asked me. "They thought I *was* a gadwall."

As with the Mallard Drake Call, we were the first company to introduce a gadwall drake call. Gadwalls are about the same size as mallards, but there's really nothing very distinctive about them. The male gadwall is gray-brown with a black patch at its tail, while the females are patterned with brown and buff. The male gadwall makes short, deep, reedy calls that sound like a burp; the females quack like mallards, but with a higher pitch. To call a gadwall, you give the call one *tat* every four seconds or so.

Unlike the gadwalls, wood ducks are very distinctive. They're the only ducks that perch and nest in trees—they have sharp claws—and they're comfortable flying through woods, hence their name. They also have a unique shape: they're boxy with crested heads, thin necks, and long, broad tails. The males have glossy green heads with white stripes, burgundy breasts, and buff sides. The female wood ducks are gray-brown with white-speckled breasts. The male wood duck has a thin, rising and falling whistle that sounds like *jeeeeee*; the female makes a loud *oo-eek, oo-eek* sound when flushed and screams *cr-r-eek, cr-r-eek* to sound an alarm.

Keith Powell, who was one of my first employees at Duck Commander, built our first wood duck call out of wood. It has a short little reed in it, and you use your tongue to manipulate the sound. The key to calling wood ducks is you never want to use a flying call when the real ducks are flying. There's a different call for sitting, and that's the one you want to use when the ducks are in the air. If you're flying and the real ducks are flying, then everyone is flying and no one knows where to land. If you call them to sit, they'll swim right up to your blind so you can shoot 'em!

## HAPPY, HAPPY, HAPPY

During the evolution of Duck Commander, we've built duck calls from wood, plastic, polycarbonate, and acrylic. We now have single-reeded calls, double-reeded calls, triple-reeded calls, and even reedless calls. We even have some calls today that are injection molded! Our calls come in a variety of colors and styles, but each call is still assembled by hand and custom tuned to make sure it sounds like a duck. If it doesn't sound like a duck, it's fixed or thrown into a pile of rejects. Jase, Jep, Si, John Godwin, Justin Martin, or one of a slew of other folks tests every duck call in the assembly room in our warehouse. I think our quality control is what separated our products from our competitors' a long time ago.

In the beginning, I was quality control. Even though we had the best product on the market, it took a while for sales to really pick up. In the late 1970s, I began to notice that Walmart stores were popping up in a lot of the small towns where I was doing business. Before too long, I noticed the hunting and fishing, sporting goods, and hardware stores that had previously bought my duck calls were closing their doors. I knew if I didn't find a way to get my products into Walmart, I wasn't going to be in business for very long either.

So one day, I pulled my old truck in front of the first Walmart I saw, walked in, and said, "Hey, how many of these duck calls do you want here?"

"Duck calls? You mean, off the street?" the lady behind the counter asked me.

"Yeah, yeah," I answered mildly, noting her resistance.

The clerk laughed and told me, "We don't buy any duck calls. Son, you need to go to Bentonville."

"Bentonville?" I asked her, knowing Walmart's corporate headquarters was several hours away in Arkansas. "Nah, I've just got some duck calls right here."

The clerk firmly told me no thanks and brusquely sent me away. So I drove on down the road and pulled up to the next few Walmart stores I saw. I changed my pitch a little bit to try to get someone interested, playing my tape and blowing my calls to show how they worked. Finally, one of the store managers told me, "I'll tell you what. You got an order form?"

"Nah, I don't have an order form," I told him. "I just figured you could pay me out of petty cash back there in the back of the store somewhere."

"Well, I've got a three-part order form I need to fill out," he said. "I'll tell you what; I'll try six of them."

When the store manager filled out a three-part form with WALMART at the top of it and wrote down "six duck calls," I walked outside looking at my copy and thought, *I've got me something here.* Well, when I got to the next Walmart thirty miles down the road, I showed the store manager the form and told him, "Walmart's stocking these duck calls. This last store ordered six."

He said, "Give me what you've got."

That was the beginning of our Walmart business. Using the same technique, I amassed a stack of order forms to show and prove to managers of Walmart stores across four states that other stores were buying our duck calls. I eventually built the business, as our sales loop grew wider, to where we were selling $25,000 worth of calls to Walmart each year.

Then one day our phone rang, and the voice on the other end said, "I need to talk to Mr. Robertson."

"Yeah, that's me," I answered.

"Are you the one who's getting duck calls into Walmart stores?" the man asked me.

"Yes, that's me," I told him.

"Son, let me ask you a question," he said. "How did you get duck calls into the Walmart chain without going through me?"

"Well, just who are you?" I asked.

"I'm the buyer for Walmart!" he screamed.

There was a pause.

"One store at a time," I told him.

There was a long pause.

"Let me get this right," he said. "You

> "How did you get duck calls into the Walmart chain without going through me?"

mean to tell me you've been driving around in your pickup truck and convincing our sporting goods departments to buy duck calls without even conferring with me, who's supposed to be doing the buying for the whole Walmart chain?"

"Sir, I didn't mean to slight you or anything," I said. "Look, I didn't even know who you were. Bentonville's a long way. I'm just trying to survive down here!"

He thought about that for a minute, then said, "I'll tell you what I'm going to do. Anybody who can pull a stunt like that, I'm going to write you a letter authorizing you to do what you've been doing."

"Man, I appreciate that," I told him.

"I'm going to authorize you to go into our stores," he said. "You'll have that letter from me, and that makes it all aboveboard."

"Hey, I'd appreciate any help you can give me," I said.

So the buyer in Bentonville wrote me a letter and sent it to me. I got the letter and showed it to every store manager I met. They all told me, "Come on in, Mr. Robertson."

Our business with Walmart really started growing then. About a year or two later, with sales steadily accelerating, I called the buyer. "Look," I said, "it's a computerized world. We can probably speed this thing up if you buy a certain amount of my calls per store." The buyer told me to come to Bentonville and meet with him. He agreed to buy our calls and distribute them to

Walmart stores, an action that eliminated a lot of our workload and expanded the sale of duck calls into new areas of the United States. Together, we eventually built the account to sales of more than $500,000 per year—big numbers for Duck Commander, but relatively small for Walmart. Our profit from the sales put us on solid ground financially and provided the base for our future growth.

Things went on that way for about twenty years, but then Walmart began to scale down its waterfowl hunting business. Only about one million people in the United States hunt ducks. There wasn't enough money in it for a company that measures its customer base in multiple millions. We were making what we considered to be pretty good money, but it wasn't enough for Walmart, which deals in billions of dollars. The duck calls had always been more of a customer service for the company. So, basically, they got out of the duck-call business.

Fortunately, we had expanded our business into other stores, like Cabela's, Bass Pro Shops, Academy Sports + Outdoors, and Gander Mountain, so we were no longer as dependent on one big contract like Walmart. The specialty hunting stores were not only buying our duck calls, but they were also stocking our hunting DVDs, T-shirts, hats, and other hunting gear. The independent hunting stores have long been some of our most loyal clients and are still a big part of our business today. Without them, we never would have gotten off the ground. Although we reestablished our business relationship with Walmart a few years later, Duck Commander was able to survive and prosper during the years in which we didn't do business with the world's biggest retailer.

Duck Commander has been making hunting DVDs for more than two decades, although the first ones were actually filmed on VHS tapes. I watched a lot of deer-hunting and big-game-hunting TV shows, and I was convinced there was a market for waterfowl-hunting videos when perhaps no one else was. No one had really tried it with ducks, and I was certain we could do it better than anyone else. I rented camera equipment from a company in Dallas and hired Gary Stephenson, a science teacher at Ouachita Christian School, to film our first video. As with our duck calls, not a lot of other people believed my videos would be a success. In fact, Jase told me he was absolutely certain no one would watch them! *Duckmen 1: Duckmen of Louisiana* was released in 1988 and sold about one hundred copies. I set out to film *Duckmen 2: Point Blank,* which took us the next five seasons to produce. We didn't know anything about making movies, and I had no idea it would take us so long to make a second hunting video.

> Jase told me he was absolutely certain no one would watch my videos!

But I knew it was only a matter of time until people started noticing our videos. They were fun to watch! *Duckmen* hunting tapes were unlike what anyone else was doing at the time. We were blowing ducks' heads off in slow motion and flipping deer in the swamp. The videos lasted about an hour each and were among the first to include rock music over hunting scenes. I have always been a big fan of classic rock. I loved Lynyrd Skynyrd, Led Zeppelin, Creedence Clearwater Revival, Pink Floyd, and Bob Seger. Lynyrd Skynyrd is definitely my favorite. If there's one rule at my house, it's that you never wake me while I'm napping. If you wake me before I'm ready, there's going to be heck to pay. One day, one of the members of Lynyrd Skynyrd called the Duck Commander office, wanting to talk to me. I was taking a nap at home, and the receptionist at the office was under strict orders not to wake me, so she took a message. I was so mad when I found out. I told everyone, "From this day forward, wake me up if the president of the United States or Lynyrd Skynyrd calls!"

> I told everyone, "From this day forward, wake me up if the president of the United States or Lynyrd Skynyrd calls!"

More than anything else, the *Duckmen* videos put a face to our company. I had a long beard and so did most of the other original Duckmen—Mac Owen, Dane Jennings, and W. E. "Red Dawg" Phillips. Red Dawg was the first one to paint his face in the blind so the ducks wouldn't see him. He couldn't grow a long beard like the rest of us, so he figured he'd paint his face to look different. After a while, I figured out paint was the best way to camouflage our white faces from the ducks. Nothing stands out like a white surrender flag in a duck blind more than a white man's face! Now everyone in my blind is required to wear face paint. People grew to love our DVDs; I think there was a shock factor involved, and people wanted to see what the crazy Cajuns in Louisiana would do next! In 2012, we released *Resurrection: Duckmen 16.*

The hunting DVDs ended up being a lot like our duck calls—we didn't hit a home run in our first at bat, but we kept going back up to the plate. Eventually, the hunting DVDs caught on and became popular enough to help Willie land us a show on Outdoor Channel, which led to even bigger things with *Duck Dynasty* on A&E. Even though Duck Commander faced difficult times and what seemed liked insurmountable obstacles, we stayed the course and never gave up. I've always believed that if we did what was morally and ethically right, while continuing to steadfastly believe in what we were doing, we'd end up okay in the end. As long as we gave our best, continued to build products we believed in, and never strayed from God's purpose for us, I knew Duck Commander would find a way to persevere. It's what the Robertson family has always seemed to do.

# REDNECK CAVIAR

*Rule No. 11 for Living Happy, Happy, Happy*
Suck the Head of a Crawfish
(You'll Want to Do It Again and Again)

After living more than six decades on Earth, I have reached the conclusion that ducks are the most protected species on the planet. In the United States of America, ducks are the most protected and overly regulated entity in history. It's amazing how many rules and regulations our government puts on duck hunters. (If you don't believe me, check with the U.S. Fish and Wildlife Service's website for all the up-to-date information.)

To even hunt ducks, I have to begin on a precise day at an exact minute, which is pretty difficult for a man who has never even owned a watch! I can't fire a shot until thirty minutes before the sun comes up, so I have to constantly look to see when the sun is going to rise and then deduct thirty minutes to determine when I can fire my first shot. Of course, the sunrise and sunset are constantly changing, depending on the rotation of Earth. But I always have to be aware of when the sun is going to come up because there might be a game warden sitting out there with a watch, waiting to write me an expensive ticket.

The U.S. government also dictates that I can have only three shells in my shotgun at once, not four or five, which would be a lot more efficient. I also have to have a precise kind of metal shot in my shells. It can't be lead; it has to be steel so it's not harmful to the ducks or the environment.

Where I live in eastern Louisiana, we are allowed to hunt ducks for sixty days each year. This past season, the first split of duck season started on November 17, 2012, and lasted sixteen days. After a two-week hiatus, duck hunting commenced again on December 15, 2012, and lasted forty-four days, until January 27. The government also tells me how many ducks I can kill—no more than six per day. But I also have to know what species of ducks I kill—I can't shoot more than four mallards, two pintails, three wood ducks, etc.—and I have to know the sex of the ducks whose lives I've ended. If I wing a duck—shoot it down and cripple it, but don't kill it—I have to make a reasonable attempt to find it or I'm in violation of federal law. I'm telling you: it's the rule book of all rule books when it comes to duck hunting. Unborn babies don't have as much protection in this country!

Here's the government's most silly rule: if I have a good day in the blind and want to give my buddy or a neighbor a few ducks to eat for dinner, I can't do it without documenting what I gave them. I have to write down my hunting license number, date of birth, legal name, physical address, and telephone number, and then specify how many ducks I'm giving them, what kind of ducks I'm giving them, and what sex of ducks I'm giving away. It's just one thing after the other when it comes to duck hunting.

Here's another dilemma: the law says I can kill six ducks per day for sixty days in the Mississippi Flyway. I was never very good in math, but I believe that comes out to three hundred and sixty ducks per season. But another federal law says I can only have a maximum of twelve ducks in my possession at once. Okay, let's see now, one law says if I start on opening day and kill six every day, I can shoot down three hundred and sixty ducks in a season. But the other law says I can't have more than twelve in my deep freezer, so the government apparently wants me to eat 'em as soon as I shoot 'em. Now, we like to eat duck more than most people, but the average duck weighs about one pound when it's dressed. The government expects me to eat three hundred sixty pounds of duck in sixty days? What am I supposed to do with the ducks that I can't eat? Feed them to my dogs?

If I'm ever elected president of the United States—and you never know—the first thing I'm going to do is downsize the Department of the Interior. I don't know of any politician who has ever said he would do that. I'd also make sure we have plenty of nesting ground for ducks, so I'd work with our friends in Canada, where most of the ducks are born. I'd take all the money we're sending to the Middle East, where we're trying to pay people to be our friends, and divert it to Canada and earmark it to help raise ducks. We don't need to be sending money to the Middle East; too many of those people are mean. The Canadians are already our friends, and Canada would be number one on my list for foreign aid. So when I'm elected president, we're going to lower taxes and make sure we give the Canadians truckloads of cash to raise mallard ducks. The American people are tired of pork-barrel spending; let's spend some money on ducks!

> If I'm ever elected president of the United States— and you never know—the first thing I'm going to do is downsize the Department of the Interior.

The bottom line is the U.S. government doesn't have to be so strict about duck hunting. In my opinion, it only needs to educate people about what you can shoot and what you can't shoot. It's a great sport, but it would be even greater if there weren't so many rules and regulations.

Of course, I've always been of the opinion that I've been given permission from headquarters to shoot and kill whatever animals I want. According to Genesis, God instructed Noah to build an ark to save himself, his family, and a remnant of all the world's animals after God decided to destroy the world because of mankind's evil deeds. God instructed Noah to build the "ark of cypress wood; make rooms in it and coat it with pitch inside and out." God told Noah to "bring into the ark two of all living creatures, male and female, to keep them alive with you. Two of every kind of bird, of every kind of animal and of every kind of creature that moves along the ground will come to you to be kept alive."

After Noah did what God told him to do, the floodgates of the heavens opened on the seventeenth day of the second month, and rain fell for forty days and forty nights. The earth was flooded for one hundred and fifty days. As Genesis 7:23 tells us, "Every living thing on the face of the earth was wiped out; people and animals and the creatures that move along the ground and the birds were wiped from the earth. Only Noah was left, and those with him in the ark."

When the floodwaters finally receded, Noah and his family left the ark. According to Genesis 9:1–3: "Then God blessed Noah and his sons, saying to them, 'Be fruitful and increase in number and fill the earth. The fear and dread of you will fall on all the beasts of the earth, and on all the birds in the sky, on every creature that moves along the ground, and on all the fish in the sea; they are given into your hands. Everything that lives and moves about will be food for you. Just as I gave you the green plants, I now give you everything."

# HAPPY, HAPPY, HAPPY

Now, I'm not a man of great intellectual depth, but it sounds to me like God Almighty has said we can pretty much rack and stack anything that swims, flies, or walks, which I consider orders from headquarters. I have permission from the Almighty to shoot whatever I want! Of course, I'll follow whatever rule or regulation the government puts in place. My days as an outlaw have long been over.

I really wonder if the U.S. government has any idea of the cost and work it takes to get ducks to fly to my land in the first place. At last count, we had fifty-four duck blinds on about eight hundred acres of our land. As Duck Commander grew and became more profitable through the years, Kay and I had a little bit of money to invest, and we decided to buy land. What I wanted was something I could feel, touch, and stand on—something tangible. When the stock market collapsed a few years ago, a lot of the young bucks came to me crying about all the money they lost on Wall Street. I never could figure it out. They said their money was in a brokerage account they could see on a computer, but then it was gone. Where did the money go? It didn't disappear. Someone had to take it. Where is it? That's why I invest in something tangible like land—no one can take it from me.

Our first purchase was a plot of forty acres in the wetlands near our house. We bought it, then added more land through the years, until we accumulated what we have now. Mac Owen, a longtime hunting companion of mine, who appears in many of the *Duckmen* videos, also wanted to get in on the investments. Together Mac and I bought surrounding land as it came up for sale—usually forty acres at a time.

Our investment has paid for itself many times over, primarily because the land we purchased was the most feasible and economical place for oil and gas companies to cross the Ouachita River with their pipelines. The fees we collected from the utility companies were more than triple what we paid for the land. I also bargained with the companies to ensure that the duck habitat would not be damaged. In the end, the pipelines were laid in a natural-looking curve. I think the plan may even have enhanced the area's appeal to ducks because I mow the pipeline right-of-way regularly, eliminating brush and encouraging more grass to grow.

We have planted, cultivated, and protected the grasses on our land primarily for ducks. Our wetlands are covered with native millets, sedges, and nut grass, as well as planted stands of Pennsylvania smartweed, American smartweed, and sprangletop, creating a mosaic of wild and cultivated plants. They are all prime foods for wildlife. The grasses are heavy producers of the seeds on which ducks thrive. Millet is one of the best foods available for ducks. In a good year, smartweed can produce more than five million seeds per acre. Ducks love them, and their craws are often found stuffed with the small black seeds. Sprangletop is another heavy seed producer; some of its seeds will remain edible for as long as seven years.

That the grasses also sustain crawfish is a bonus. Everything eats crawfish at every stage of a crawfish's life: fish, birds, raccoons, bullfrogs, snakes, turtles, large water beetles, and humans. Crawfish are a Louisiana delicacy, and we've harvested them to eat and sell. Crawfish are also an important ingredient in the swamp ecosystem, so I do everything I can to propagate them.

Shortly after we bought the land in the wetlands, I observed all of the water leaving through one low drainage area on the edge of our land. The water dumped into a creek before emptying into the Ouachita River. To control the water depth on our land, I built a low levee across the area. I marked the highest level the water reached on trees, which allowed me to determine how high and long to make the levee. As I was building it, I installed a forty-eight-inch culvert through it at the lowest spot, and then put a weir, or gate, across it to control the water depth. I can adjust the water depth of the wetlands six inches at a time simply by adding or taking out a top board from the weir.

I regulate the flooding of my land in accordance with what crawfish require—which, coincidentally, meets the needs of mi-

Crawfish are an important ingredient in the swamp ecosystem, so I do everything I can to propagate them.

grating ducks as well. The crawfish normally hatch in October, when the rains return. They grow through the winter, reaching adulthood in March. Hopefully, enough rain will fall to refill the area. If the area isn't filled naturally, I use a big pump to draw water from the river. Normally, I have to do some pumping to ensure that most of my land is covered with water to a depth of twelve to eighteen inches—ideal for both the crawfish and duck populations. The depth is determined by how far a duck can stretch its neck to feed when it bobs underwater. After duck season is over, I drain the land to promote the growth of grasses and trees.

After we purchased the wetlands, a Louisiana Fish and Wildlife Department survey showed that 65 percent of the timber in the area was bitter pecan trees, which can grow as tall as one hundred feet. The wood is not as desirable as hickory or regular pecan, but it is resilient and is used to make such things as axe and hammer handles. The worst thing about bitter pecan trees is that they drop pignuts, which taste so bad that most wildlife won't eat them. I set out to eliminate the bitter pecan trees and replace them with oak trees that would produce more palatable fare for a wider variety of wildlife—including both squirrels and deer, which love acorns.

It turned out to be a formidable task. After the bitter pecan trees were cut and sold, the following year suckers began to sprout from all the stumps. Left alone, multiple tree trunks would grow from the stumps, and the area would be reforested with bitter pecan trees, thicker than before. So I got a lawn trimmer, the kind with a blade, and went from stump to stump, one at a time, and mangled off all the sprouts. Then I treated the stumps with poison to finish killing them off. It took me three years to clear them all.

Then I was thinking about how to get the area seeded with oaks. I had planted and seeded many oaks and cypress trees but was still working on it when the Almighty stepped in and flooded everything in the area in 1991. The water picked up acorns and deposited them over all the area I'd cleared. When spring came, there were thousands and thousands of oaks of all kinds, sprouting every foot or so. It was a blessing from above, and while the flood destroyed the home where Pa and Granny were living and its water rose to the front steps of our house, the floodwaters provided us the now heavily wooded areas where we hunt today.

About 90 percent of your success in duck hunting is determined by the location of your duck blind, and we've made major improvements to water conditions, soil conditions, and how natural feed gets to the holes we're hunting. I've kept detailed records of every one of the hunts on our land for more than two decades, including specifics about weather, wind direction, types of ducks we saw, and the position of the sun. It's amazing to look back and see how much better the hunting has been over the last few years after the improvements were made.

For instance, on opening day of the 1995 duck season, we hunted Dog Bayou, a blind on my land, and we killed one mallard, seven teals, and one ring-necked. A few days later, we hunted the Dog Bayou and didn't even fire our guns. Good night; we stayed until two o'clock in the

> I've kept detailed records of every one of the hunts on our land for more than two decades.

afternoon and didn't kill a duck! During the 1995 season, we killed 266 ducks in 60 days. Now we try to average twenty ducks per day between four or five of us in the blinds. During the first split in 2012, we killed more than two hundred ducks in the first ten days. We've gone from two hundred ducks in 1995 to more than one thousand ducks now.

The crazy part is we can make as many improvements as we want to our duck blinds, but they'll never be as good as the ancestral holes. Some of the land next to mine used to be a swamp, but the owners leveled it in the 1960s and turned it into rice fields. Some guys got in a duck blind over there and noticed that ducks kept flying to one particular spot on the field. They asked the farmer why ducks were sitting there, and he told them it's where a lake used to be. The trees and the water are gone, but the ducks are still flying there because it was where the lake once was. It's in their genetic makeup to fly there.

It's one of the phenomena of Mother Nature that can't be explained through science. There are a lot of them, and the only explanation I can come up with is that God is in charge and has a blueprint for how everything works. Take, for instance, the Arctic tern, a medium-sized bird, which is famous for flying from its Arctic breeding grounds to Antarctica and back every year, covering more than 43,000 miles round-trip. The terns travel down the coast of Brazil or Africa to get to their wintering ground every year. Some evolutionists want us to believe that the reason they fly to Antarctica every year is because once upon a time one tern found its way there, told some terns about it, and then they all started going there. Makes a lot of sense, doesn't it?

I, for one, believe the terns were born knowing they had to fly to Antarctica every winter to survive. To prove the point, researchers once robbed a tern's nest and raised the little birds away from their mother. Then they banded them when they were old enough to fly. The terns had never seen Antarctica and had never been around another tern to tell them to fly there. So when it was time for the terns to fly south, the researchers flew over the Arctic Ocean and dropped them from an airplane. The terns made one circle and then flew south, arriving in Antarctica a few weeks later.

Why would they do that? Because there were about twenty different life forms that relied on the terns to survive. The Arctic fox couldn't survive without its eggs, and certain plants and worms couldn't live without its droppings. Hawks couldn't survive without feeding on the birds. The terns were part of the food cycle in both the Arctic Ocean and Antarctica.

The ducks that fly south from Canada each year and winter throughout Florida, Louisiana, Texas, parts of Central America, and beyond are the same way. Everything from alligators to snapping turtles to skunks rob ducks' nests and eat their eggs. Foxes, coyotes, and birds of prey eat their babies when they're young. Humans hunt ducks, too, and they put meat on our tables. It's the Almighty sending literally millions and millions of pounds of protein from one end of a continent to the other end, feeding all of these things along the way.

> The Almighty sends literally millions and millions of pounds of protein from one end of a continent to the other end, feeding all of these things along the way.

It's like the mayfly on the river. A mayfly starts out as a larva in the water and looks like nothing more than a little maggot. When the water level rises, the larvae crawl up the trees on the riverbank. They build cocoons that look like spiderwebs and then emerge as flying creatures. You see mayflies flying all over the river and they live only long enough to drop their eggs into the water. Why? Because when they die and fall into the water, fish come up and eat them. Mayflies are fish food! It's a cycle: mayflies drop their eggs and then they die, fish eat them, the larvae climb up the trees, and then it starts all over again. Who's feeding the fish? The Almighty is feeding the fish.

God is feeding everything, including you and me, and a lot of us in His ecosystem eat us some crawfish.

# PRODIGAL SONS

*Rule No. 12 for Living Happy, Happy, Happy*
Learn to Forgive (Life's a Lot Easier That Way)

The good Lord blessed Kay and me with four healthy, obedient sons, each of whom grew up to become a godly man who loves his wife and children and shares God's Word through his work with Duck Commander and in our church. But I'm not sure I needed to see how they came into this world! A few weeks before our youngest son, Jeptha, was born in 1978, Kay informed me she wanted me at the hospital to witness his birth.

Now, I didn't want to be in the delivery room when Jep was born. When our oldest son, Alan, was born, I wasn't there and he turned out fine. I wasn't there when Jase came, but everything still turned out okay. When Willie came next, I didn't want to press our luck, so I didn't go to the hospital again (in fact, I was fishing when he was born). But when Kay became pregnant with

Jep, she told me it was the last baby we were going to have, so she wanted me beside her to witness God's greatest miracle. Women being the strange creatures they are, Kay decided she needed a coach for the birth of her last child, and she insisted that I was the one to do it.

When the day arrived for Jep's birth, Kay decided she was going to deliver him without an epidural or any kind of medication. I knew then that I had a tough woman! Over the next several hours, I watched my wife thrashing around and gritting her teeth, and then I saw Jep's head emerge from my wife's loins. Let me tell you something: I salute womanhood worldwide, because women are exceptionally tough for enduring the misery of childbirth. I've cleaned hogs and gutted deer, but in my experience on Earth I've never witnessed such a brutal event.

I knew right then that my sex life was over—although I somehow managed to get over my concerns thirty days later! Let me put it to you this way: after going through it once, I'd never go back and do it again. It was rough to watch, so I can't imagine having to experience the pain. If men were in charge of carrying and birthing our babies, we'd have a lot fewer people on Earth, because we'd only do it once—I can promise you that!

Each of our boys was a blessing, and after I repented and had my life in order again, I set out to give them the same sort of childhood I had as a boy, learning to hunt and fish and live off the

land. Alan, Jase, and Willie were very close when they were growing up, and then they kind of took Jep under their wings after he
was born because there was such an age gap between them. My
philosophy on discipline was very simple. Since rules are made to
be broken, I kept the rules few and far between. However, there
was a code in the Robertson house: three licks was the standard
punishment. It wasn't ten licks or twenty licks for doing something wrong; it was always three: thump, thump, thump! It was
a principle, and my boys always knew what their punishment
would be if they stepped out of line.

They received three licks if they disrespected their mother. As
it says in Ephesians 6:1–3, "Children, obey your parents in the
Lord, for this is right. 'Honor your father and mother'—which is
the first commandment with a promise—'so that it may go well
with you and that you may enjoy long life on the earth.'" I never
had to tell my boys not to disrespect me; that rule was understood
and it never crossed their minds to break it. None of my sons ever
disrespected me, not even once. Nobody ever bowed up and told
me I wasn't going to tell them what to do.

There was literally flawless obedience when they were living under my roof—at least when I was home. If I told them to
go to bed, they jumped up and went to bed. If I told them to
rake the leaves, they raked the leaves. If I told them to clean the
fish, they cleaned the fish. People would come over to visit us

and were amazed at how obedient our sons were. Their teachers always told us our boys were among the most well-behaved students in school. I believe it's because my boys were always aware of the consequences of not doing what they were told to do. They always respected me, and they respected their mother because I didn't want them taking advantage of the woman who put them on Earth.

I also didn't allow my sons to fight with each other. They could argue and disagree all they wanted—and Jase and Willie managed to do it regularly. I didn't have a problem with them raising their voices at each other to make a point. I wanted to encourage them to argue and make a case for their beliefs. But if it came to blows and there was meat popping, they were getting three licks each. I didn't care who threw the first punch. If it ever came to physical blows, I'd step in and everybody involved got three licks.

Another thing I didn't allow was tearing up good hunting and fishing equipment. I wanted them to respect someone else's property and to be thankful for what we had, even if it wasn't much. If one of the boys borrowed one of my guns or fishing poles and tore it up while they were using it, they received three licks. I always wanted my boys to have access to my guns to hunt, just like I had access to Pa's guns when I was growing up. When I was young, I knew if I broke a gun, we probably weren't going to eat that night because we were so dependent on wild game for food. But since my boys knew there was going to be a meal on the table every night, they weren't always as respectful of my equipment. When Alan was about fourteen, he and a few of his buddies borrowed all of my Browning shotguns to go bird-hunting. They were hunting on a muddy track and because they were careless and immature, mud got into a few of the shotgun barrels. They were very fortunate the guns still fired and didn't blow up in their faces! When Alan returned home, he was so scared to tell me what happened to my Browning shotguns—my Holy Grails—that he enlisted Kay's help to break the news. I'm sure Alan thought I was going to beat him on the spot, but I simply told him to go outside. I was afraid to whip him right then because I was so angry. After cooling off, I pulled Alan and his buddies together and gave them a stern lecture about gun safety and respecting other people's property. I also told Alan—after I gave him three licks—that he was on probation from using my guns for a long time.

There was another time when I discovered that one of my boat paddles was broken. None of my boys would fess up to doing it, so I gave each of them three licks. It was kind of a military-style group punishment. It turned out that one of their buddies actually broke it, but he didn't confess to the crime until several years later. I'm sure he realized that if he'd confessed when the boys were younger, they all would have whipped him!

# HAPPY, HAPPY, HAPPY

As hard as Kay and I worked to instill morals, principles, and a belief in what's right and wrong in each of our sons, it wasn't always easy. People might watch *Duck Dynasty* and sometimes think we're the perfect family. They see how much we love and respect each other. But the reality is that it wasn't always easy. We had our trials and tribulations like every other family out there, and there were actually times when Kay and I believed we would lose more than one of our sons. They were the scariest times of our lives.

> As hard as Kay and I worked to instill morals, principles, and a belief in what's right and wrong in each of our sons, it wasn't always easy.

Alan, our oldest son, probably had the roughest childhood because he was the oldest boy when I was having all of my problems. Kay was essentially a single mother for a long time, so Alan was given a lot of responsibility when he was only a young boy. When Kay started working at Howard Brothers Discount Stores, Alan was only seven but was left at home to care for Jase and Willie. Alan had to grow up really fast and didn't get to enjoy his childhood or play baseball and other sports like his brothers did, at least not until I turned my life around. Alan also attended four or five different schools because we moved around so much, which I'm sure wasn't very easy for him either.

## Prodigal Sons

Alan was a very popular kid in high school, and before long he was hanging out with the wrong crowd. I can remember one time when he and some buddies were camping at a spot down the road from our house. They were drinking beer and did some foolish things, like knocking down mailboxes along the road. Some neighbors came to our house the next morning to complain about it, and I jumped in my truck to find them. I brought Alan and his buddies back to our house and lined them up against my truck. I gave each of them three licks. There was one boy I didn't even recognize, but I told him if he ever wanted to come back to the Robertson house, he was getting three licks like the rest of them!

After Alan graduated from high school, his behavior was so wild and out of control that Kay and I didn't want him around his younger brothers anymore. He was the oldest boy and his brothers looked up to him, but he wasn't setting much of an example for them. So we threw Alan out of our house, which certainly wasn't an easy thing to do. My sister Judy was living in New Orleans at the time, and Alan moved there to live with her. You want to talk about going from the frying pan to the fire!

Alan lived in New Orleans for about two years, and he started dating a woman. She told Alan she was divorced, but she was really only separated from her husband. The husband followed Alan home from work one day and beat him really bad with an iron tire tool. When a policeman showed up at the scene and talked to Alan, he could sense there was something different about him.

"Son, where are you from?" the policeman asked Alan.

"West Monroe, Louisiana," Alan told him.

"I don't know what went wrong in your life and how you ended up here, but go back to wherever you're living. Pack up everything you've got, and go back to your mom and dad. I can tell you're a good boy and just got off track."

Alan told me he looked up at the police officer, as the sun was shining behind him, and he looked like an angel. Alan believed the police officer was sent by God to help him turn his life around.

Alan came home and we greeted him with open arms. We cooked a big meal and celebrated his homecoming. It was like the Parable of the Lost Son in the Bible. In Luke 15:11–24, Jesus tells us that there was a wealthy man with two sons. When the younger son asked for his share of the estate, the man divided his property between his two sons. Before too long, the younger son left for a foreign country and squandered his wealth through unrighteous living. Then a severe famine wiped out everything, leaving the younger son homeless and hungry. After briefly working as a swine herder, the boy repented and returned home to his father:

# Prodigal Sons

*While he was still a long way off, his father saw him and was filled with compassion for him; he ran to his son, threw his arms around him and kissed him. The son said to him, "Father, I have sinned against heaven and against you. I am no longer worthy to be called your son." But the father said to his servants, "Quick! Bring the best robe and put it on him. Put a ring on his finger and sandals on his feet. Bring the fattened calf and kill it. Let's have a feast and celebrate. For this son of mine was dead and is alive again; he was lost and is found."*

The incident in New Orleans helped Alan turn his life around. He worked for Duck Commander for a few years, then attended seminary and worked as a pastor at White's Ferry Road Church in 1988, eventually becoming a senior pastor there. While Alan is still heavily involved in the church and often preaches on Sunday, he rejoined the family business in 2012. He helps maintain our schedules and travels with me to speaking engagements and other appearances around the country. Alan has a calming effect on everyone around him, and he's really good at defusing situations. He's the one who rides herd around his brothers and is the voice of reason and wisdom among them. Alan and his wife, Lisa, have two daughters. His oldest daughter, Anna, has been working with Duck Commander since high school. Her husband, Jay, who was a teacher and coach at a high school, started working with us building duck calls during the summer, but now he's with us full-time.

Unfortunately, we also had to go through some of the same struggles with Jep as he grew older. When Jep was in high school, he was the only boy living at home because his brothers were married and living on their own. The older boys like to say Jep had it a lot easier than they did growing up. I was still pretty strict on the boy, but our business was doing a lot better, so he probably had a few more luxuries than the older boys did.

I'll never forget one night Jep was coming home late and got his truck stuck in a muddy road close to where we live. It was in the late 1990s, so Jep had one of the early cell phones in a bag in his truck. It was after midnight, and he called home and Kay woke me up to get Jep out of the mud. I had a Jeep that I bought brand-new in 1974, but it was pretty old by then, and the lights didn't work anymore. I usually only drove the Jeep to my duck hole and back. So I had Kay follow me in her car to provide lights for me to see. It was still raining pretty heavily when we got to the field where Jep's truck was stuck. I jumped out of my Jeep to winch his truck out, but then Kay pulled up right next to me, not realizing she'd driven into the soft mud! Now Jep was stuck in front of me, and Kay was stuck behind me. "I am surrounded by idiots!" I screamed.

Jep went all the way through middle school without having any problems, and then we sent him to Ouachita Christian School, which was pretty expensive. We figured if he went to high school there, he wouldn't get into any wild stuff. But with only four or five months of high school left, Jep broke up with his girlfriend. And then he started sailing backward. I couldn't believe it and didn't want to believe it, to be honest. He moved into an apartment in West Monroe with his cousin, who was attending college at the University of Louisiana–Monroe. Just like Alan, Jep started drinking, cutting up, and using drugs. We knew Jep was drinking because we could smell alcohol on his breath at church on Sunday if he'd been out drinking the night before. Kay would always ask me, "What's that smell?" I'd tell her, "That's whiskey on Jep's breath."

> Just like Alan, Jep started drinking, cutting up, and using drugs.

Willie was actually the one who brought the seriousness of Jep's problems to our attention. Willie was working with the high school youth group at White's Ferry Road Church, and he found out Jep had asked one of the kids to go to a bar with him. Willie came to our house and said, "I'm done. We've got to do something right now. I'm just tired of it." We called Alan and decided to have a family intervention. Alan lined everything up, and we were all waiting for Jep when he came to the house one night. Kay was terrified because she was certain I was going to throw Jep out of the house, like I'd done with Alan.

I told Jep, "Give me the keys to your truck—the one I'm

paying for." He pulled the keys out of his pocket and handed them to me. I told Jep what his brothers had told me about his behavior.

"Son, you know what we stand for," I told him. "We're all trying to live for God. We're not going to let you visit our home while you're carrying on like this. We're paying for your apartment. We're paying for your truck. You've got a decision to make. You're either going to come home and basically live under house arrest because we don't trust you, or you can hit the road—with no vehicle, of course. Somebody can drop you off at the highway and then you'll be on your own. You can go live your life; we'll pray for you and hope that you come back one day. Those are your two choices."

Jep looked at me, lowered his head, and started pouring out his sins to me. He said he'd been taking pills, smoking marijuana, getting drunk, and on and on. He was crying the whole time, as he confessed his sins to us and God.

I'll never forget what Jep said next. He looked up at me and asked, "Dad, all I want to ask you is what took you so long to rescue me?"

After Jep said that to me, everyone in the room was crying.

"You still have a choice," I told him.

"Well, my choice is I want to come home," he said.

Jase has always been our most straitlaced son, so he was the hardest on Jep when he strayed.

"Son, you can't hang out with those people," Jase told him.

"Daddy won't let 'em get to me," Jep said.

"Daddy won't and we won't, either," Jase promised him. "But you have to come to all the good things to help you. You've got to find better friends. You can't be running around. You have to break it off with the bad influences."

Thankfully, our second prodigal son was coming home. It was a heart-wrenching episode for all of us. Alan was so distressed by his little brother's struggles that he left our house, drove down the road, and then stopped and dropped to his knees and wept in a field.

Like Alan, Jep turned his life around after overcoming the struggles of alcohol and drugs. He came to work for Duck Commander and found his niche as a videographer. He films the footage for our Duckmen videos and works with Willie on the Buck Commander videos. Jep is with us on nearly every hunt, filming the action from a distance. He knows exactly what we're looking for in the videos

> Alan was so distressed by his little brother's struggles that he left our house, drove down the road, and then stopped and dropped to his knees and wept in a field.

and films it, downloads it, edits it, and sends it to the duplicator, who produces and distributes our DVDs.

Having worked with the crew of *Duck Dynasty* over the last few years, I've noticed that most people who work in the film industry are a little bit weird. And Jep, my youngest son, is a little strange. It's his personality—he's easygoing, likable, and a lot more reserved than his brothers. But he's the only one who will come up to me and give me a bear hug. He'll just walk up and say, "Daddy, I need a hug." The good news for Jep is that as far as the Duck Commander crowd goes, one thing is for sure: weirdos are in! We covet weirdos; they can do things we can't because they're so strange. You have to have two or three weirdos in your company to make it work. It's truly been a blessing to watch Jep grow and mature and become a loving husband and father. He and his wife, Jessica, have four beautiful children.

Like I said earlier, Jase was the only one of our four sons who stayed the course and never deviated to the right or left. He always looked straight ahead; he never drank, never cursed, and always lived his life the way God wanted him to live. I think one of the reasons Jase and Willie never strayed too far is because they were so involved in the youth group at White's Ferry Road Church. Willie's only problem was that he believed he was a ladies' man until he met Korie. He was always jumping from one girl to the next until he settled down. It really made an impact on both of them. Jase was always looking out for his brothers. Even though Jase and Willie were very competitive growing up, Jase always had Willie's best interests at heart. One time, Willie and Jase were at a friend's house in high school. Jase walked into the basement and found Willie playing strip poker with some other kids.

"What are you doing?" Jase asked him.

"Playing strip poker," Willie replied.

"You've stripped enough," Jase told him. "Let's go."

The thing I really like about Jase is that he's as obsessed with ducks as I am. I rarely took my boys hunting with me when they were very young. In fact, I never took them when I was still an outlaw. "Not this time, boys, we might be running from the game warden," I'd tell them. But after I repented and came to Jesus Christ, I started taking my sons hunting with me, beginning with Alan. Before we moved to where we live now, it was a pretty long haul from town to the Ouachita River bottoms. Alan got carsick nearly every time I took him hunting, but he didn't think I knew. We stopped at the same gas station every time, and he'd walk around back and lose his breakfast before he climbed back into the truck. I was proud of him for never complaining.

I took Jase hunting for the first time when he was five. He was shooting Pa's heavy Belgium-made Browning twelve-gauge shotgun, which he could barely even hold up. It kicked like a mule! The first time Jase shot the gun, it kicked him to the back of the blind and flipped him over a bench.

"Did I get him?" Jase asked.

I knew right then that I had another hunter in the family, and Jase is still the most skilled hunter of all my boys. I trained Jase to take over the company by teaching him the nuances of duck calls and fowl hunting, and he is still the person in charge of making sure every duck call sounds like a duck. Not only did Jase design the first gadwall drake call to hit the market, he also invented the first triple-reed duck caller. Jase and I live to hunt ducks. We track ducks during the season through a nationwide network of hunters, asking how many ducks are in their areas and what movements are expected. Then we check conditions of wind and weather fronts that might influence duck movement. We talk it all over during the day and again each morning, before the day's hunt, as we prepare to leave for the blind.

When Kay and I began to ponder becoming less active in the Duck Commander business, we offered its management to Jase, who had been most deeply involved in the company. But he had no desire to get into management. Jase likes building duck calls and doesn't really enjoy the business aspects of the company, like making sales calls or dealing with clients and sponsors. Like me, Jase is most comfortable when he's in a duck blind and doesn't care for the details that come with running a company. Jase only wants to build duck calls, shoot ducks, and spend time with his family (he and his wife, Missy, have three kids).

So then we offered the company's management to Willie, who seemed to have the most business sense among our sons. I knew from the time Willie was only a little boy that he could sell beachfront property in Iowa if he put his mind to it. When I was a commercial fisherman, Willie sold fish on the side of the road with Kay or me. Willie can still quote some of the sales pitches: "Yes, sir, these are golden buffalo, the pride of the Ouachita River." Willie was even selling carp, a worthless fish you couldn't sell at the fish market, but he was able to unload quite a few of them with his salesmanship and charm. Willie always said if you can sell fish, you can sell anything. He sold candy from his locker while he was in elementary school and sold worms from an old wooden boat on our river dock. The boy always knew how to make a dollar.

Willie attended college at Harding University in Searcy, Arkansas, and then finished up at Louisiana-Monroe. He gained some management experience from working at Camp Ch-Yo-Ca, a Christian youth summer camp, where he met his wife, Korie, whose family owned the camp. They were married shortly after Korie left for college and now have four children.

Willie, at age thirty, agreed to take over Duck Commander.

For the first few months, he cleaned the yard around my house and did other odd jobs while he learned the business. Before too long, Willie convinced me he was capable of doing a lot more. He became involved in the business side of the company, expanding our Internet operations (Korie's dad, Johnny Howard, was selling our merchandise through a catalog and online before she and Willie bought the operation) while also landing us new sponsors and endorsement deals. Willie also landed the company its TV deals with Outdoor Channel and then A&E, which really put Duck Commander in the fast lane.

In 2005, Kay and I sold majority interest of Duck Commander to Korie and Willie, and Willie became the company's CEO. I have to admit he took Duck Commander way past anything I could have done with it. They purchased a thirty-thousand-square-foot warehouse in West Monroe, which was previously the storage space of Howard Books, which Korie's family also owned. They moved Duck Commander's operations from my house to the warehouse. They also simplified and computerized the company's bookkeeping and accounting, which Kay had handled for years, and made it more efficient.

Willie also gets credit for making flowing, untrimmed beards the standard appearance for Duck Commander employees. In a lot of ways, he became the new face of the company. I couldn't be prouder of him. He's taken the company where I never thought it could go. He's a great businessman, and he's a heck of a hard worker. He's a visionary, and he had a vision for what Duck Commander could be. I call him Donald Trump II because he's a deal-maker and knows how to network in the hunting industry.

With Willie in charge, it was easy for me to walk away from Duck Commander. When Willie and Korie took over the company, I told them, "Y'all take care of the company and send me my check every month. As long as the checks keep coming, I'll know y'all are doing well. I'll stay in the woods, and as long as a check comes in the mailbox every month, you won't hear anything from me." I don't go to the Duck Commander warehouse very much anymore. I'm not often up there sticking my nose into their business. A lot of old guys who start businesses and then turn them over to their children want to hang around and can't let them go. Not me. When I told them to take it over and run with it, I meant it and have left them alone.

> Willie also gets credit for making flowing, untrimmed beards the standard appearance for Duck Commander employees.

The thing that has probably pleased me the most about Duck Commander since Willie took over is that it's still a family business, just like when I started the company. Heck, you basically have to have Robertson blood in your veins to get a job there! Jase, Jep, Willie, and Si are still very involved in the day-to-day operations of Duck Commander, and now Alan is back in the fold, too. Now all of my boys have come home to where it started.

Through all of our trials and tribulations, Kay and I have realized that raising a family is about love and forgiveness. Our boys weren't perfect growing up, but they always had an anchor—our faith in Jesus Christ—and that helped us get through our struggles. As it says in Proverbs 22:6 (KJV): "Train up a child in the way he should go: and when he is old he will not depart from it." My boys might have strayed from God's path for them at times, but they always had their faith to fall back on. If you don't have faith, there's nowhere to turn. My boys always knew where to go when they ran into trouble.

# RIVER RATS

*Rule No. 13 for Living Happy, Happy, Happy*
Share God's Word (It's What He Asks of You)

For the first twenty-eight years of my life, I didn't know the gospel and I didn't know Jesus Christ. Now I'm trying to make up for lost time. Jesus said all the authority was given to Him, and He told us to go preach the gospel and make disciples of all the people we baptize. Basically, Jesus is telling me to go forward and share with people what I didn't know until I was saved. So I've been sharing everything I've learned since I was converted. Nowadays, I get asked to speak to churches, colleges, hunting clubs, and other groups around the country. The Almighty has put me on the road, but some of my best work still occurs on the Ouachita River right in front of our house.

When I was still a commercial fisherman, I sometimes had over one hundred hoop nets and trotlines stretching all the way across the Ouachita River. But these pirates on the river kept stealing my fish. Now, people have been shot in Louisiana for taking fish out of someone else's nets or off their trotlines—which might make sense when you realize someone's livelihood is being stolen.

When I saw people stealing my fish, I'd run them down with my shotgun and scare the daylights out of them. It didn't do much good, though, and they kept stealing from me. But I kept scaring them, and I was making enemies up and down the river. People were probably saying, "That ol' sucker down there is about as mean as a junkyard dog."

I kept reading and studying my Bible, while the stealing continued unabated. I read Romans 12:17–21, where it says:

> *Do not repay anyone evil for evil. Be careful to do what is right in the eyes of everyone. If it is possible, as far as it depends on you, live at peace with everyone. Do not take revenge, my dear friends, but leave room for God's wrath, for it is written: "It is mine to avenge; I will repay," says the Lord. On the contrary:*
>
> *"If your enemy is hungry; feed him;*
> *if he is thirsty, give him something to drink.*
> *In doing this, you will heap burning coals on his head."*
>
> *Do not be overcome with evil, but overcome evil with good.*

I read the verse and sat there thinking, *There ain't no way that's going to work. No way! Be good to them. But, Lord, they're stealing from me!* But then I had a revelation: *Hey, wait a minute! I've never tried that. I keep running them off with a shotgun.*

It honestly made no sense to me, but I was going to try the Lord's way. So I decided the next time I saw someone lifting one of my nets, I would initiate the biblical way of dealing with them. I was going to be good to them. Sure enough, I walked out one day and heard a motor running. I looked and saw some guys pulling up one of my nets. I stood there and watched them for a few minutes. My boat was parked right on the riverbank, and I took off running and jumped in it. I had my shotgun with me. I was going to try God's way, but my faith

> It honestly made no sense to me, but I was going to try the Lord's way.

was still a little weak, so I had my shotgun as insurance! I was going to try to be good to them, but if they wanted to get mean, I was going to have to survive.

So I ran out on the river, and these guys were still coming up with my nets. I cruised right up on 'em. They saw me coming, dropped the net, and threw the float back into the water—and started fishing.

"Hey! What are y'all doing?" I shouted.

"We're just trying to catch a few fish," one of them told me.

"What were you doing with that net in your hand?" I asked him.

"Well, you know," he said as he started to stutter and mumble. "What is that? Is that what that is?"

"Is that what that is?" I repeated. "Y'all know what's on the other end of that float!"

Then I changed my tactics. In a cheerful and exuberant voice, I shouted, "Good times have come your way!"

They looked at me, wondering exactly what I was up to. I still had my hand on my Browning A5 shotgun.

"What?" one of them asked.

"Good times have come your way," I said again. "I'm going to give 'em to you. You were going to steal my fish. Evidently, you've planned a fish fry, but y'all aren't catching any. But you want a fish fry. Since you didn't catch 'em, you're going to steal 'em. Well, here's the good news: I'm going to give you what you were trying to steal—free of charge."

"Nah, we were just going to—" one of them started to say, but I cut him off.

"Nope, you want a fish fry," I said. "We're going to have us a fish fry. How many people you got coming?"

I reached over and grabbed the rope on the net and told them to keep their boat right there. "Let's see what y'all were fixing to catch," I said.

I raised my net up and looked in it.

"Whoo! Y'all would have done pretty good," I said.

By then I'm sure they figured I was certifiably nuts.

"I've got a lot of fish in here," I said. "Get your boat over here."

They started paddling and were watching me, probably to make sure I wasn't going to shoot them. I dumped the fish from my net into my boat and told them to bring their boat closer. I began throwing even more fish into their boat.

"What about this big white perch here?" I asked them. "I'm probably supposed to throw him back. What do y'all think?"

"Nah, we'll keep 'im," one of them said.

The fish kept hitting the bottom of the men's boat, and they kept watching me throw them over. Finally one of them protested mildly, saying, "I think that's probably enough."

"Look, you start frying fish, and kinfolk will start showing up who haven't been around in months," I told them. "Let's make sure you have enough."

So I threw all of my fish into their boat.

"Now! Y'all got plenty," I said.

"Yes, sir, that's plenty," one of them replied.

"Now, here's the deal," I told them. "Why steal something if you can get it for free?"

"Man, look, we're sorry," one of them said.

"I understand," I said. "Look, I live right over there. From now on, just come up there if you aren't catching anything. I'll give y'all the fish. That way, you won't have to steal. You'll get your fish. You're happy. Everybody's happy, happy, happy."

I let the net back down into the river and said, "Good to see y'all."

The men pulled away in their boat and started motoring down the river. They had plenty of fish. They were looking back at me, probably thinking, *Is this guy for real?* Maybe they remembered I had a shotgun and were about half-scared, but I never saw them again.

After that episode, everyone quit stealing from me. Every time I saw someone eyeing my nets, I'd offer 'em free fish. I was giving away less fish than what was previously being stolen from me.

I reread the texts from Romans 12 and thought, *You know what? I get it.* What the Almighty is saying is that no matter how sorry and low-down somebody might be, everybody's worth something. But you're never going to turn them if you're as evil as they are. If you're good to them, you might appeal to their conscience—if they have any conscience. Now, there are some people who might be so mean you probably can't be good to them. But most people are perplexed after someone is good to them when he should have been mean. Most of the time, they end up giving up their evil ways.

The Almighty was right—as He always is. The incident on

the river had a profound impact on me. From that point forward, I wanted to help others, whether it was by sharing the gospel and baptizing them, giving them fish, or assisting them in any way possible. Over the past twenty years, my sons and I have literally led thousands of people to Jesus Christ. Alan, Jase, and Willie are ordained ministers and attended seminary at White's Ferry Road Church. Often, after one of us speaks at a church or somewhere else, as many as one hundred people

> What the Almighty is saying is that no matter how sorry and low-down somebody might be, everybody's worth something.

will come forward, expressing their desires to become Christians. Many visitors to my house walk down the hill with us to be baptized at the boat launch—sometimes even at night, with car headlights illuminating the scene.

One of the first opportunities I had to speak to a large crowd was at the Louisiana Superdome in New Orleans in the early 1990s. I was invited to speak and demonstrate duck calls during a hunting and fishing show. I had a crowd of about one thousand people listening to me, and I blew my calls and gave them some hunting tips. Then I reached into my bag and pulled out a Bible. I told them, "Folks, while I'm here, I think I'm gonna preach you a little sermon." I thought I owed it to them to share the gospel.

"I'm standing under a sign that says, 'Budweiser is the king of beers,' and everybody's got their beers here today," I told them. "But I'm here to talk about the King of Kings. I know I might look like a preacher, but I'm not. Here's how you can tell whether someone's a preacher or not: if he gets up and says some words and passes a hat for you to put money in, that's a preacher. This is free. This is free of charge, which proves I'm not a preacher."

I preached for about forty-five minutes, and afterward several men came up and thanked me for sharing my story. A few of them even invited me to preach at their churches, so that's kind of how my road show started. I like to think of myself as a guerilla fighter for Jesus. Because of the success of *Duck Dynasty,* I'm getting more opportunities to speak to larger audiences now. But I don't care if I'm talking to one person or one thousand; if I can help save one lost soul and bring him back to Jesus, it's well worth it to me.

The good Lord leads us to lost souls in many different ways. We meet some of them at our speaking engagements, others at church, and some simply stop by the house. I'll never forget the time when someone called my house to order duck calls, back when Duck Commander was still being run out of our living room. The man kept using the Lord's name in vain during his conversation with me.

"Let me ask you something," I told him. "Why would you keep cursing the only one who can save you from death?"

There was silence on the other end.

"You got my order?" the man asked.

"Yeah, I got your order," I told him.

Click. He hung up the phone. A few minutes later, the phone rang again.

"Mr. Robertson, I've never thought about what you said," the guy told me.

"Well, you ought to," I told him. "Let me ask you something: Where are you from?"

"Alabama," he said.

"You're about ten hours away," I said. "You ought to load up and head this way. I'll tell you a story about the one you've been cursing."

About a week later, there was a knock on the front door. This young buck stepped in the house and asked, "You know who I am?"

"I don't reckon I do," I told him.

"I'm that fella from Alabama who was cursing God," he said.

The man had a buddy with him, and I told them the story of Jesus Christ. By the time I was finished, they were on the floor crying like babies. I took them down to the river and baptized both of them that night.

I remember another time when I gave a duck-call demonstration at a sporting goods store. True to my homage to the Almighty, I blew on some duck calls and then preached from the Bible. When I was finished, I concluded with what I always tell my audience: "Where else can you go on a Friday evening in America and get first-rate duck-call instruction and a gospel sermon at the same time?"

Well, about five years later, a guy who was there wrote me a four-page letter. He said he went to the sporting goods store to listen to a duck-call guru because he wanted to become a better duck hunter. However, he wasn't prepared to listen to what I had to say about the Bible, about how we're all sinners and we're all going to die. He thought I'd taken advantage of him. When the man went home, he burned every one of my duck calls and for the next several years told anyone who would listen to him that I was the sorriest, most low-down man he'd ever met.

He shared that story on the first two pages of the letter he sent me, but I didn't hold it against him and kept on reading. On the third page, he told me he woke up one morning and realized he couldn't get what he'd heard out of his mind. He couldn't forget me telling him that God loved him, his sins had been paid for, and that he could be raised from the dead. After a couple of years of romping on me so badly, he asked himself why he was so mad at someone who loved him enough to tell him that story. So he picked up a Bible and started reading it himself. It confirmed everything I'd told him. He told me his wife was thrilled, his kids were happy, and they were a much closer family now. He felt guilty because he thought I knew he'd been poor-mouthing me, which, of course, I didn't, and wanted to apologize for being an idiot.

Here's the point of his letter: if you really love someone and want to tell them about what God's done for us, there's no way to escape without being persecuted. I usually tell anyone I talk to that I'm going to share the gospel because I love them. I tell them it's not contingent on how they feel about me. If they hate me, I'm not going to hold it against them. If they don't like me, they can walk away. But I have to love my enemies. If anyone has a better explanation as to how I can be resurrected, I'm open to listening to new ideas. I'm all ears when it comes to an alternative, but I've never found another way in which I'm going to make it out of here alive. I don't know any other way, so I'm sticking with what I know to be the gospel.

The man who wrote me the letter was baptized and saved, but he went down kicking and screaming. Most of the other people we've converted over the years have accepted Jesus Christ as their savior more willingly. For about twenty years, we had Bible study at our house on a weekday night and house

I'm all ears when it comes to an alternative, but I've never found another way in which I'm going to make it out of here alive.

church on Sunday nights. One time, Jep and his best friend, Trey Fisher, brought eighteen teenagers to the house, and we baptized every one of them that night in the river.

We were never really sure what we'd find on the riverbank when we walked down for a baptism. One night, we took about twenty people down to the river to take their confessions and baptize them. About the time we were ready to walk into the water, a couple of rednecks pulled up in their boat. It was obvious they'd had a couple of beers to drink.

"What the hell is going on around here?" one of them yelled.

"I'll tell you what," I said. "We just preached the gospel to these people, and we're gonna baptize 'em right here. You all want in on the action?"

I ain't never seen a motor crank up that fast and leave!

Our dogs always seemed to follow the crowd to the river for baptisms. I was baptizing a young man one time, and just as soon as I pulled him out of the water, the dogs started fighting for some reason. Without skipping a beat, I told the young man he must have had an evil spirit in him, which God had miraculously transferred to the dogs! There were about ten dogs squealing and barking, and I told him the dogs were going to fight the demon out of them! The funny part is everyone on the riverbank thought I was telling the truth!

We conducted another baptism at our house one night

when the river was really high, which brings water up close to our house, along with the snakes, alligators, and other dangerous debris. My boys went out with flashlights and shotguns to clear our path; they were always on sentinel duty when we baptized someone at night. In fact, during a baptism one very dark night, I accidentally stepped off the normal path and led us into an alligator or turtle bed, and we both disappeared into the water. I like to think that baptism was a twofer!

A lot of the people we've converted over the years have become our very close friends and some of them were even married in our front yard. We've probably conducted a dozen weddings at our house, with Alan officiating most of them. Paul Lewis was Willie's best friend growing up. Paul received a full scholarship to play basketball at Southeastern Louisiana University in Hammond. He even played against Shaquille O'Neal one time and seemed to have a very bright future. But in 1995, Paul was arrested for transporting drugs in Texas and was sentenced to fourteen years in federal prison. He ended up serving twelve and a half years, which was a hard lesson to learn, and Willie was at the prison to pick him up the day he was released.

Willie gave Paul a job at Duck Commander, where he met his future wife, Crystle, a former Texas police officer. They both rededicated their lives to Jesus Christ and were married in our front yard. Paul is African-American; Crystle's mother is Hispanic and her father is black. So the wedding crowd consisted of African-Americans and Hispanics but mostly white, bearded rednecks. About the time the wedding proceedings were starting, a friend of mine was putting his boat into the river at our boat dock. My friend later told me he realized then that there must be a God, because every other time he had seen so many ethnicities together, there was usually fighting involved! But there, under the towering pines and oaks next to Cypress Creek in our front yard, he saw a lot of people from different backgrounds who seemed to genuinely love each other and were enjoying being around each other. It was a perfect picture of what Christ's body should look like on Earth. My family and I are proud to create scenes like that one as a witness to what we believe.

Whenever I think of all the people we've baptized over the years, I always recall a conversation Jep had with one of his buddies in the backseat of our car when he was really young. Jep's friend Harvey asked him what it meant to be a Christian.

"Well, when you get to be about thirteen or fourteen years old, my daddy will sit you down and study the Bible with you," Jep told him. "He'll make sure you know what he's talking about. And then he'll tell you that Jesus is going to be your Lord and when that happens, you can't act bad anymore. My daddy will ask you if you want Jesus to be your Lord. If you say yes, we're all going down to the river. We'll be so excited that we'll be skipping down there. My daddy will put you under the water, but he won't drown you. He'll bring you back up and everybody will be clapping and smiling. That's what he'll do."

Nowadays, you don't see many families—the husband, wife, and children—that are so evangelistic. I think it's pretty rare in today's world. The thing that pleases me most about my sons is that no one ever told them to do it. They just decided to be that way. Maybe it was handed down when they heard me telling Bible stories and saw me baptizing people in the river. I didn't have Jesus in my life until I was twenty-eight. But during the last thirty-eight years of my life, I've been telling everyone I meet about him. It was a big change for me. I was converting people to Christianity even before I started

> "My daddy will put you under the water, but he won't drown you."

making duck calls. Then came the business, the blessing, and the fame, but I've stayed the same throughout. Everywhere my sons and I go, we're telling people the good news about Jesus, blowing duck calls, and making people happy, happy, happy—then down the road we go.

# FOUNDING FATHERS

*Rule No. 14 for Living Happy, Happy, Happy*
Read the Bible (We Can Still Save This
Once-Great Country—It's Not Too Late)

After I became a Christian, one of the first changes I made in my life was to take a more active interest in politics and how our government works. I'd never voted until I was twenty-nine, but I decided I ought to do so in order to help put godly men and women in positions of authority—instead of a bunch of heathens—since God works through people.

After studying several political parties to find out what they believe and stand for, I decided my political ideology was more in line with the Republicans. I definitely was no Democrat—that's for sure—but I don't really consider myself one or the other. I'm more of a Christocrat, someone who honors our founding fathers and pays them homage for being godly men at a time when wickedness was all over the world. Our founding fathers started this country and built it on God and His Word, and this country sure would be a better place to live and raise our children if we still followed their ideals and beliefs.

I'm worried about the United States of America, there's no question about it. There's wickedness all over our country. America is a country without morals and principles, and it's a far cry from the great nation our founding fathers created in 1776. Great men like George Washington, Thomas Jefferson, and Benjamin Franklin, who signed the Declaration of Independence and whom you see on our money today, agreed that God and the Bible would be their moral compasses for constructing the greatest nation on Earth. But now we've taken the Bible out of schools, we've taken the Ten Commandments out of courtrooms, and stores like Walmart aren't even allowed to publicize Christmas anymore! What kind of country are we living in nowadays?

It really seems pretty simple to me. We're in the year A.D. 2013 We've been counting time by Jesus for more than two thousand years. He must have done something right! In his Thanksgiving Proclamation in New York on October 3, 1789, Washington, the very first president of the United States, said, "Whereas it is the duty of all nations to acknowledge the providence of Almighty God, to obey his will, to be grateful for his benefits, and humbly to implore his protection and experience." I'm with George Washington. It was Jefferson, our third president, who said, "All men are created equal." Man didn't crawl out of the ocean like some of these evolutionists would like us to believe; Jefferson believed men were *created* equal. He also said, "We hold these truths to be self-evident, that all men are created equal, that they are endowed by their Creator with certain unalienable Rights, that among these are Life, Liberty and the pursuit of Happiness." Those are God-given rights, folks. I'm with Thomas Jefferson.

Sure, our founding fathers weren't perfect, and they made mistakes along the way. They allowed slavery to take place in our country for close to a hundred years and didn't allow women to vote in the beginning, but we as a people atoned for our mistakes and corrected them. The difference between our founding fathers and the cats that are ruining our country today is that men like Washington and Jefferson created the greatest country on Earth and these modern-day politicians didn't!

In a letter to several governors of the first states, Washington wrote, "I now make it my earnest prayer, that God would have you, and the State over which you preside, in his holy protection." There it is; is that the last time you heard one of our politicians offer a meaningful prayer to God Almighty? The only thing today's politicians want to talk about is separation of church and state, but our founding fathers wholly embraced their Creator.

Jefferson, the principal author of the Declaration of Independence, could speak ten languages and was studying French,

Latin, and Greek when he was nine. When John F. Kennedy, our thirty-fifth president, brought together the Nobel Prize winners at the White House in 1962, he told them, "Ladies and gentlemen, I think this is the most extraordinary collection of talent, of human knowledge, that has ever been gathered together at the White House, with the possible exception of when Thomas Jefferson dined alone." That's how much respect and admiration JFK had for Jefferson. And why wouldn't he? Jefferson authorized the Louisiana Purchase from the French and it turned out to be a pretty good deal!

Jefferson was a smart cat, and his fears about America's future are sadly coming to fruition. Jefferson once famously said, "To take from one, because it is thought that his own industry and that of his father's has acquired too much, in order to spare to others, who, or whose fathers have not exercised equal industry and skill, is to violate arbitrarily the first principle of association—the guarantee to every one of a free exercise of his industry and the fruits acquired by it." Jefferson warned us that socialism would ruin the American democracy, and look what's happening in our country now. Today, our government is saying the democracy will thrive if you take from those who are willing to work and give to those who aren't. I have to pay more taxes so that everything can be free for those people who don't want to work? It's nonsense. Our government is doing exactly what Jefferson warned us against. So the question is, who is right? I think Jefferson was on the right side.

Jefferson also said, "It is incumbent on every generation to pay its own debts as it goes. A principle which if acted on would save one half the wars of the world." What is our national debt now? More than $16 trillion, and it's climbing every minute with no debt ceiling in sight. We made a grave mistake and didn't pay our debts as a country as we moved forward. Once you don't pay, you dig a never-ending hole like the one we have now. Look at the financial disaster we're leaving our future generations. Our children and grandchildren are going to be saddled with debt up to their eyeballs! My reading of history has convinced me that most bad government comes from too much government. Ronald Reagan, our fortieth president, once famously said, "As government expands, liberty contracts." Right again!

You know what Jefferson had to say about the health care programs our government is trying to force down our throats? He said, "To compel a man to furnish contributions of money for the propagation of opinions which he disbelieves and abhors, is sinful and tyrannical." We shouldn't have to pay for stuff we hate, and I don't want to pay for a health care program that endorses legalized abortions. No one has the right to make us pay if we don't want it. Now, the government is saying we have to pay for programs like health care, whether we like it or not. It's sinful and tyrannical, according to Jefferson.

Jefferson also warned us to make sure we maintain our right to bear arms. He said, "No free man shall ever be debarred the use of arms." Jefferson was telling us, "Boys, make sure you keep your guns." In a democracy, the strongest reason for the people to retain their right to keep and bear arms is as a last resort to protect themselves against tyranny.

Jefferson was one of our first presidents, so you'd think the first thing he'd want to do is confiscate everyone's guns. But he actually said the opposite and believed that if things ever went south, the people were going to need their guns. That's pretty serious talk, but that's what Jefferson said. Washington agreed with him and basically said firearms are America's liberty teeth. In his first message to Congress on the State of the Union on January 8, 1790, Washington said, "A free people ought not only to be armed, but disciplined." Do you see their point? It's by the people, for the people, Jack!

John Adams, our second president, said, "Statesmen . . . may plan and speculate for Liberty, but it is Religion and Morality alone, which can establish the Principles upon which Freedom can securely stand." Adams told us that if we don't have God in our lives and aren't morally righteous, we're going to lose it all. That's where we are now, and I fear that's what's fixing to happen.

## Founding Fathers

Now we can't figure out what's wrong with America's youth. Our children are plagued by violence, alcohol, drug abuse, teenage pregnancies out of wedlock, and high dropout rates. Well, Noah Webster, who is considered the father of American education, basically believed that the Bible was America's basic textbook in all fields. In his *History of the United States,* Webster wrote, "The most perfect maxims and examples of regulating your social conduct and domestic economy, as well as the best rules of morality and religion, are to be found in the Bible." Webster must have been a pretty intelligent guy, because I'm still using a *Webster's Dictionary*! But we're not even allowed to start the school day with a prayer or have a Bible in a classroom. Webster believed you had to vet everything through the Bible. We got away from it and now we're paying the price. We should have listened to Webster.

What are we going to do with our youth? How are we going to reduce crime? How are we going to prevent our children from having babies? What are we going to do? The only solution our government can come up with nowadays is to pour more money into our problems and research solutions. Webster said what we need to do is put the Bible back where it ought to be. I'm right there with him!

> Webster must have been a pretty intelligent guy, because I'm still using a *Webster's Dictionary*!

# HAPPY, HAPPY, HAPPY

Without the Bible as a blueprint for living our lives, I'm not surprised to see our country struggling so mightily. Romans 1:28–32 says:

> *Furthermore, just as they did not think it worthwhile to retain the knowledge of God, so God gave them over to a depraved mind, so that they do what ought not to be done. They have become filled with every kind of wickedness, evil, greed and depravity. They are full of envy, murder, strife, deceit and malice. They are gossips, slanderers, God-haters, insolent, arrogant and boastful; they invent ways of doing evil; they disobey their parents, they have no understanding, no fidelity, no love, no mercy. Although they know God's righteous decree that those who do such things deserve death, they not only continue to do these very things but also approve of those who practice them.*

The apostle Paul was writing about the Roman Empire, but he might as well have been talking about present-day America. We fought Operation Desert Shield and Operation Desert Storm in the early 1990s, and then we continued to fight in Afghanistan and Iraq for more than a decade to weed out terrorists. According to the U.S. Department of Defense, we lost nearly seven thousand brave soldiers during those wars. But there's a bigger war going on in America. According to the Centers for Disease Control and Prevention, over sixteen thousand people were murdered in the United States in 2010. While a good chunk of our firepower was in the Middle East trying to get a handle on terrorism, we were losing an even bigger war right here in the good ol' USA. Sadly, our children are the ones doing a lot of the killing.

I'm extremely worried about our country's youth. Remember the scene from *Duck Dynasty* when I joined my grandson on a date with his girlfriend in my boat? I told him, "Son, no hands below the neck." What was I trying to tell him? My greatest fear is for one of my grandchildren to come up and tell me they have herpes. Don't you think it a little ironic that what follows sexual immorality is herpes, chlamydia, AIDS, syphilis, and gonorrhea? How could something as much fun as sex all of the sudden bring these horrible diseases upon us? Doctors have been researching these diseases for centuries, but they can't cure most of them. They can't get rid of most of them. What do you call that? You call that the consequences of disobeying the Almighty.

Look, you're married to a woman and she doesn't have AIDS, chlamydia, syphilis, gonorrhea, or any of the rest of them. Here's the good news: you don't have it and she doesn't have it. Guess who is never going to get it if you keep your sex right there? The only way it can be transmitted to you or your spouse is if you go out and disobey what the Almighty says. When it's one woman and one man, you won't catch this stuff. But if you disobey God, His wrath will be poured out upon you. It's not a coincidence that horrible diseases follow immoral conduct—it's the consequences that follow when you break God's laws.

# HAPPY, HAPPY, HAPPY

During the 1960s, I was involved in a lot of the sins I'm talking about. Remember, before I was converted when I was twenty-eight, I was running with the depraved crowd. I've been there and done that. I'm sorry to say it, but my generation gave itself over to sinful desires and sexual impurities. Thankfully, it's not too late to save our next generation.

What in the world ever happened to the United States of America, folks? Our country is so different from the nation that was founded more than two hundred years ago. I'm absolutely convinced that the reason America went so far and so fast is that our founders were God-fearing men. It was godly from the start. Our founding fathers fled the wickedness of Europe and came to America to build a nation built on principles, morals, and their beliefs in Jesus Christ. They drew upon their faith and biblical ideals to actually construct the framing documents of our great country.

The irony of it all is that we're right back to what they ran from 237 years ago. We're right back to old King George. Our forefathers' greatest fear was that the very thing they revolted against would come full circle and we'd be right back to where they started. When Webster was asked what the greatest thing that ever passed through his mind was, he said it was his accountability to God. I agree with him wholeheartedly. I'm not going askew from the principles on which the United States was built;

## Founding Fathers

I'm right there with our founding fathers. I'm a patriot and a Christian, and I'm moving forth with what they started. But now it's gotten to where I'm some kind of nut or Bible beater.

I say, so be it. I'll still go across the country spreading God's Word, like I've done since I was twenty-eight. I may be only one man reading Scripture and quotes, carrying his Bible, and blowing duck calls to crowds, but, hey, it has to start somewhere. It's what makes me happy, happy, happy.

# LETTERS FROM THE FAMILY

## A NOTE FROM ALAN

Out of the many memorable lines and quotes I have heard from my dad through the years, the one that always seems to stand out the most is "Son, don't ever tell people how good or great you are at something; let them tell you." For a man who has achieved his own level of greatness in the eyes of so many, those words were both prophetic and wise. To be the best at anything, one has to have a lot of confidence and a certain amount of ego and drive. But one must also have humility to make a life-changing impact on people. I realize now that that is what Dad was teaching me all those years ago. Of course, to become a legend, one that other people admire and want to emulate, you also have to add faith and dedication to what you love. A good woman doesn't hurt either.

My mom has always been Dad's biggest cheerleader, from

when he was a high school quarterback to when he became a Christian to when he faithfully plunged into this dream that is now known as Duck Commander. Her humility and dedication held them together when he was not the man he needed to be, and now she keeps him humble as his right hand and soul mate. Believe me, there would be no Duck Commander legend without Miss Kay!

What I respect most about my dad is that he allowed and continues to allow God to guide him. He offered himself to the Creator and humbly accepted a path that has now led to fame, recognition, and greatness, but has led mostly to glory to God and a life change for thousands of people. What I respect most about my mom is that she never gave up on him. Through her love for God and us boys, she led Dad to his relationship with God and changed all of our destinies. Their motive for Duck Commander has always been Kingdom first.

From my perch as the oldest son, I have had the opportunity to see the longest and greatest impact Dad's life change and legacy have had on our earthly family, our forever family, and the world we live in. I have also personally experienced his love and support throughout my days here on Earth, even when some of those days were dark and I didn't want to listen to him or Mom. I have grown and flourished as a man and as a man of God because of the influence of my parents, and I am forever grateful for them.

I thank my mom for her tenacity, long suffering, and close friendship. She taught me how to forgive and see potential goodness in people that others cannot see. She taught me that hope is one of God's greatest virtues when things seem dark and difficult. I thank my dad for his guidance, commitment to God, and visionary faith. He saw what we couldn't, and he has taught me to appreciate what can be done when others say it cannot be done. He taught me how to work hard and achieve your dreams. He taught me to appreciate God's creation through a love of the outdoors and the simple beauty in the smallest things. From a smartweed stalk to a crawfish hill to a buttonwillow thicket, Dad has always seen the hand of God in the nature that surrounds us. He also taught me that people are worth loving because God made us to be loved and to share a message of love and redemption.

My dad would follow his own advice and never tell you how great he is, but I don't mind telling you at all.

## A NOTE FROM JASE

I'm the second son of Phil and Kay Robertson. Si (Phil's youngest brother) named me on the riverbank. Si went to the river to tell Phil that Kay was having a baby. I've always heard that Phil's response was something to the effect of, "What do you want me to do about it?" Si asked him, "What do you want to name him?" Phil replied, "Name him after you." So I was given the name

# HAPPY, HAPPY, HAPPY

Jason Silas Robertson. Maybe that's why Si and I love to argue so much. My dad called me "Jase" about half the time, and somewhere through the years the name stuck.

I was five or six when I noticed a change in my dad's life. I was probably eight when I realized this change was going to be permanent and for the better. Up until that time, my life was filled with a lot of fear. I remember seeing scary-looking people and a lot of fistfights, usually ending with the flashing lights of police cars. I just tried to stay out of the way and survive. This all seemed to culminate one night with my most vivid memory as a child. I remember being awakened in the middle of the night and having to move out with my mom and brothers at the direction of my dad.

We moved to West Monroe, Louisiana, and it seemed like an eternity before I saw my dad again. It was a few months, and I remember my dad pulling up in a cool-looking Jeep. I could tell something had happened—he was a new creation.

It was not until I was fourteen that I figured out what happened. I had gone to a Bible study and had gotten "stirred up" about this one called Jesus. I asked my dad about it, and he told me that's the same message he'd heard. Not long after that conversation, Phil and I waded into the Ouachita River and he baptized me. I then realized why he was a new creation.

The years we spent on the river were some of my fondest

memories. We commercial-fished together, hunted everything, and spent a lot of time around the table, eating what we caught and playing dominoes. I think what made it so special was that we were a reconciled family and brothers in our faith. Through this we became really good friends. He taught me how to blow a duck call and how to skin a catfish. Most importantly, he taught me how to be a godly man.

I remember countless gospel studies with all kinds of people and lots of river baptisms. I learned how to be hospitable and to value people no matter what their skin color or whether they were rich or poor. Most important for me, I learned that as a follower of Christ you could have a lot of fun. It was not so much what we were doing around the riverbank but whom we were with on the riverbank. Thanks, Dad!

## A NOTE FROM WILLIE

I'm happy I get to write about my dad when I'm older in life. The older I get, the more I'm starting to realize how great he really is. Not great because of all of his many accomplishments, but because of who he is and how he has lived his life. I know he has not always been what he wanted to be in life, but all of us have made mistakes; it's how we deal with them that makes us great or not. Dad spent much of his younger years searching for something. When he found it, he sold out for what it gave him—peace and hope. He lived his early life with neither, and I would have to say I would have done the same if I didn't know Jesus. He lived his life without peace, and he in turn gave no peace. He lived his life without hope, so he gave none as well. He lived only by what he saw. But after he accepted Jesus Christ as his savior, he learned to live by what he couldn't see. And that is what he taught me after he found it.

I find myself living more and more like my dad as I get older. It's probably because we were somewhat in the same birth order. I am the third in four children and he was the fifth in seven. We shared the same type of childhood. We both had nothing when we were young but never wanted any help and were self-made men. We had to really stand out to "stand out." Neither of us ever feared failure, and if we did, we surely wouldn't admit it. Each of us decided we would never live our lives in the trap of some man-made structure or like caged birds doing what we are supposed to do. Both of us knew at early ages that we needed a great partner to help us in life. We both put our spouses through trying times to make them prove to us that they really loved us for who we really were. And both women saw something in us that we did not see in ourselves, something that could be great with a little help and patience.

I would love to give all the credit to our gals, but without the Lord, it would have been impossible. We will bow to no man, but we bow to something bigger than us. God is the only thing that can tame the wild horse in both of us. It is as simple as that. It just makes sense to have hope beyond our lives on Earth. If the only thing we can rest on is how good life is here on Earth, then it may be comprehensible to think life ain't so bad. But I have to wonder, what if I were born somewhere else on the planet? Somewhere that wasn't so good? What if we couldn't hunt, prosper, be happy, and have such a good family? It wouldn't seem fair, would it? That is why we put our hope in something else. God's way is better.

My father went through all the bad to teach me not to do it, and I didn't. I don't have to testify about how bad I used to be. Yes, I made and continue to make bad decisions, and I am in no way perfect. I also have done many things the right way and have been a positive influence on many people. I have brought many people to the Lord and counseled teens, college kids, and married people. I have worked for the church, gone to seminary, and completed mission work. And I did most of it when I was still only a teen. I don't deserve any glory. I simply followed the examples my parents showed me and did what my heavenly Father told me to do. The byproduct was I knew my dad would be pleased with what I was doing with my life.

My dad taught me to be a salesman, hard worker, good man, visionary, entrepreneur, problem solver, good husband, good father, and great hunter. He taught me to be independent, confident, and fearless, but most of all godly. I never remember him talking about his accomplishments on the ball field, and he never was big on homework, ball practice, or how we looked. He did, however, do what my wife said many years ago, which was to "hot-wire us to God." Not so we would make him happy, but so we would make Him happy. I always tried to do what was right not only because it would make my dad happy, but because it would make the Lord happy.

As I sit here in my recliner, watching *The Good, the Bad and the Ugly*, literally turning into my dad, my hope is that I really do turn out to be somewhat like him. I am totally confident that we will live forever and continue to be together in the after-realm. That is the hope we share. That is why we live together without fighting and arguing, and that is why we continue to work together as friends. We are happy as a family—we share in joys, work through our problems, deal with sorrows, care for each other, and always look to the bigger picture. Yes, my dad has taught me a lot. I can only try to make him happy by putting all the things he has taught me into practice. I see no bad in him, only the good. I see no mistakes, only the achievements.

My biggest achievement was to bring him some of the glory he deserved in this life. He did so much for hunting, so much for his family, and so much for so many people. My biggest fear was that people would not know how much he accomplished. I have worked hard to make the right business moves so my father would receive the recognition he deserves. I am so glad to show America that there are still families that do the right things and care for people but can still succeed in this mean ol' world. My mom tells me all the time that I am just like my dad, and she usually says it after some of my lesser moments. But I still smile and think that those are the things that were passed to me by him. My dad has passed on to his boys the essence of what he is. And it will take all four of us to show it. None of us alone can embody who he is. He is remarkable and noble. My father is a truly great man.

## A NOTE FROM JEP

I guess growing up in the Robertson household was like growing up in a lot of American households. Since I was really young, we were skinning fish, cleaning squirrels, and picking dewberries. They were everyday events. Okay, so maybe my upbringing was a little atypical. I do think I had it a little easier than my older brothers, since Dad had repented by the time I was born. I remember getting up early in the summers and going with Dad to run the nets. He would even let me drive the boat every now and again. We would take our catch back to Mom, and then she and I would take off to the fish market to sell our catch. Something about the smell of those fish markets has always stayed with me. Those places had a stench that is beyond words. I would usually find something outside to do the rest of the day, whether it was fishing, shooting bows and arrows, or building forts.

On many nights, I remember folding boxes for the duck calls we were selling. To be honest, I don't think I did nearly as many as my brothers. But I guess I chipped in here and there. My grandmother Granny would get me to go searching for night crawlers, so I could take her out perch fishing. Those were some great times, and she taught me a lot about being patient and about life in general.

As I grew to become a man, at some point I lost sight of all those life lessons my dad and grandmother taught me. At around nineteen years old, I went on a six-month drug-induced rampage that nearly cost me my life. My brother Willie knew what I was up to and got the family together to give an intervention. I'll never forget how scared I was that day when I walked in Mom and Dad's house with all my brothers sitting around. I still remember hearing my dad say, "I know you've been up to no good; how bad is it?" I broke down and told them everything. There were a lot of tears and hugs, and I've never felt the love of a family like I did that day. My dad put me on house arrest for three months, and it was probably the best time of my life. I learned how to reconnect with God and my family and get back with some true friends, who are my closest friends to this day.

I have since married the most beautiful, spiritual, wonderful woman on this planet, and we have four amazing kids. My dad has shown me through his life how to work hard to support your family, love God, and even fit in a little hunting. My dad has always been there for me in good times and bad, and I hope I can do the same for my children. I love you, Dad!

## A NOTE FROM KAY

When people dream something as a child, it doesn't always come true. But my childhood dream of what kind of man I would marry and spend the rest of my life with did come true.

I always knew my husband would be tall, dark, and handsome, but he also had to have a rugged look, as if he'd just walked out of the wilderness. He had to love the outdoors and be able to survive there if needed. I also wanted him to be able to take command of any situation when needed.

I wanted him to be a leader but with a sense of humor, too. I wanted him to work and make a living. I wanted him to be a man's man, but with gentleness and love for me and his children, and be ready to defend us at all times. More than anything else, I wanted to feel loved and protected.

What I didn't know when I found the man who filled my dreams was that I had found a diamond in the rough. It would take a lifetime to perfect that diamond on the long journey of life.

# HAPPY, HAPPY, HAPPY

Phil and I have had many good years, some hard years, a few sad years, and a lot of struggling years to get where we are now. God put us in each other's paths. It has always been a wonderful ride for me.

I have a husband who is my best buddy and friend, my lover, my Christian brother, my champion, and the person who will always be there through thick and thin.

There is no greater love than your love for God, but right under that is your love for your husband, your partner for life. One of the great tragedies I see is people not putting every effort into the foundation of their marriage. My grandmother told me that it's one man and one woman for life and that your marriage is worth fighting for. We had a few hard and bumpy years, but prayer, patience, and some suffering and hope—plus remembering an old lady's words—were what got me through the difficult times. We have given it our all for our marriage and family, and my dreams did come true. Phil is and will always be my hero!

# Acknowledgments

Thanks to my oldest brother, Jimmy Frank, for his historical excellence, vivid memory, and storytelling. Thanks to Mark Schlabach for his insight, skill, and help with writing this book. Thanks to our old friend Philis Boultinghouse for her help in editing and mostly for not being anything like Denny. Thanks to John Howard for his help in making this project come together. I thank all of those who worked hard for little or no pay helping us get started almost forty years ago. I thank Gary Stephenson for his early work in bringing our hunting exploits to the screen and many others who have helped that process all of these years. I thank all of our Duck Commander employees for their hard work and dedication and all of our great customers and fans who have given rise to this ducky phenomenon. Thanks to the Outdoor Channel and A&E for bringing our family to the airwaves of this great country. Finally, a special thanks to all of the Robertson family, all of whom live the legacy set forward in this book. To Granny and Pa, who await the great resurrection, and to my brothers and sisters and their families and especially

# Acknowledgments

to my best friend and travel buddy, Miss Kay, and to my four sons and their families. Most of all I thank my Lord and Savior, Jesus Christ, son of the Almighty God, for washing away my sins, teaching me a better way to live, and guaranteeing my eternal inheritance.

Printed in the United States
By Bookmasters